WINNING BASICS

A Story of
Leadership,
Communication
and Inspiration

Robert B. Hamilton

PublishAmerica
Baltimore

First printing

At the specific preference of the author, PublishAmerica allowed
this work to remain exactly as the author intended, verbatim, without
editorial input.

ISBN: 1-4137-9684-2
PUBLISHED BY PUBLISHAMERICA, LLLP
www.publishamerica.com
Baltimore

Printed in the United States of America

Introduction

Winning Basics is the first in a series of books about business operations. It is a business novel, a work of fiction with characters and a story line which illustrates specific business concepts. Each book in the series will examine a different topic aimed at giving the reader low-cost, high-impact ideas for improving manufacturing results, creating the best working environment, achieving results through efficient and effective communications, creating a team-based work environment, staffing and integrating new employees, and recognizing and leveraging the value of the human resources within the business.

None of the characters in this story are modeled after a specific person, though readers will relate to some of the strengths and weaknesses that each character brings to the organization.

I'd like to thank the many people who helped to ensure that Winning Basics would become a reality. Thank you to Bill Brooks, Nathan Burke, Sara Burke, Jean Hamilton, Jennifer Hamilton, Kristin Hamilton, Todd Hamilton, Karla Johnston, Mary Mahoney,

.

and Jennifer McKenzie for spending hours reading and providing feedback during the writing and editing of this book. Your challenges and your thoughts were invaluable.

A special thank you to William Greenleaf. Your insights, feedback, and encouragement throughout this effort have been appreciated. Your work as my primary editor was outstanding!

Key Characters

Brian Jones
- President and Chief Executive Officer of Amber Rose Industries
- No understanding of manufacturing
- Marketing Executive in previous job
- Many years of industry experience with an ARI competitor

Jim James
- Production Manager
- Third Production Manager in last six months
- Two months on the job with ARI
- Strong education: Engineering and Ivy League MBA
- Demonstrated successful manufacturing experience

Mary Williams
- Factory Sustaining Engineering Manager and Factory Equipment Engineering Manager
- Jim's mentor
- First non-engineering employee at ARI
- Strong knowledge of ARI's history, products, business, and factory

Patricia Stockton
- Production Supervisor
- Less than 4 months on the job with ARI

Darin Schwartz
- Production Supervisor
- Less than 4 months on the job with ARI

Jerry Brown
- Equipment Maintenance Supervisor
- Less than 4 months on the job with ARI

Table Of Contents

Winning Basics

A Story of
Leadership,
Communication
and Inspiration

Chapter 1
Monday Morning Production Meeting

Jim James felt the muscles in his neck and shoulders tensing in anticipation as he strode down the hallway toward the conference room. He hoped this morning's factory production meeting would be different. But after almost two months as production manager with Amber Rose Industries, Jim had no real reason to believe that this meeting would be any more productive than the other 36 meetings he had attended since starting his employment. Mondays were always the worst. The employees first had to explain the factory's performance on Friday, Saturday, and Sunday – and then they had to defend it.

As he rounded the last corner and approached the conference room door, Jim saw all of the usual attendees. Stepping through the doorway was Mary Williams, the factory equipment maintenance manager and the person who had been with Amber Rose Industries (ARI) the longest. Mary had been of great assistance in helping Jim to understand exactly how everything worked at Amber Rose. She had been willing to spend many hours with him discussing the company's history, the evolution of its product base, and its staffing practices, as well as company policies, procedures, guidelines, and expectations. Without Mary stepping forward and investing her time, Jim doubted that he would have been able to do his job as production manager. Mary had served as the best possible mentor for Jim.

Right behind Mary was Pat Peters, the latest in a series of quality managers. Pat gave him a quick, nervous smile before disappearing into the conference room. She had been with ARI only about three weeks, but she was an expert in her field.

Bringing up the rear was Brian Jones, the company's owner and general manager. Jim held his breath as he slipped into the conference room behind Brian, trying not to inhale the cloud of strong cologne Brian always left in his wake. What a surprise Brian had turned out to be. In the course of day-to-day interaction, he was a wildly different person than the one who had interviewed and hired Jim.

As Jim scanned the room for an empty chair, he noticed Patricia Stockton and Darin Schwartz already seated at the table. Patricia and Darin, two of the production supervisors, had not been with ARI much longer than Jim, but the predecessor who had hired them had chosen wisely. Their solid education and excellent work experience made each of them a natural for the job. They were also working well together in their efforts to manage the factory. Jim hoped they would both stay with ARI for the long term. They showed promise not only in their current roles, but also demonstrated the skills that would move them into more challenging positions in the future. Darin, in particular, seemed like a natural replacement for Jim a few years down the road.

Several engineering managers from key groups, the equipment maintenance supervisors, and Brian's secretary rounded out the attendees for this meeting. Ted Werner, the other supervisor currently on staff, was on vacation.

As Jim set down his stack of reports and settled into a chair near the window between Mary and Darin, he wondered how Darin and Patricia were always able to beat him to the production meetings. He had been talking to them in the factory not five minutes earlier.

Brian took his usual seat at the head of the table, in a chair he had added after purchasing the business. He had claimed that he needed additional back support, but Jim knew there had to be more to it than ergonomics. The chair was an enlarged version of the others in the room, standing about three inches higher and placing Brian in a position that allowed him to look down at the others seated around the table. This position also required the others to look up when they spoke to Brian. In short, the chair put Brian in a position of absolute control.

The other furnishings in Brian's conference room likewise made clear his elevated position as owner of the company. In Jim's business world experience, he had never attended daily meetings in a room that was quite so elegant or well equipped. The oval-shaped, solid mahogany table could easily accommodate twenty people. Floor-to-ceiling windows spanned one wall. Deep, off-white carpet, handmade mahogany chairs, and top-of-the-line audio-visual equipment completed the effect. Though the room had been outfitted prior to the sale of the business to Brian, he used it to his full advantage. Based on the way Brian ran these meetings, it was clear that he felt the room afforded a position of total control when dealing not only with business visitors, but also with his employees.

As usual, Jim felt his gaze drawn to the wall across from the windows. Framed, oversized versions of ARI's Vision Statement, Mission Statement, and Key Management Areas of Focus dominated the wall. Recessed ceiling lights highlighted the rich mahogany color of the frames. Each document had been printed on parchment, as if to emphasize their importance at ARI.

Jim's eyes settled on one of the Key Management Areas of Focus – number three, *Demonstrate and Develop Trust and Respect*. From his vantage point, these morning meetings never accomplished anything in that area. Jim made a mental note to ask Brian why that area of focus had been included when there were so many incidents and practices that ran counter to it. The timing for that question, however, would have to be just right – and with Brian, there never seemed to be a right moment.

As always, copies of the output reports, shipment status reports, equipment status reports, and quality reports were neatly stacked in the center of the table. Glancing around, Jim noted that virtually everyone had brought copies with them to the meeting anyway – copies which they had undoubtedly examined in great detail before the meeting. Almost every attendee had made notes in the columns of the different reports in preparation for Brian's questions. Jim knew they were all hoping they would have the right information and the right answers should Brian ask a question.

Each of them would be taking careful notes during the meeting, as well. Brian's secretary would publish the meeting minutes within 30 minutes of the end of the meeting, but everyone wanted to be sure they had enough information around their specific open issues and assignments to bring the right data to the next meeting. They would want to be well prepared with those details when they were asked to provide updates. Many meetings had been halted so Brian could interrogate attendees who had failed to have the right answers ready.

Jim focused his attention on the head of the table as Brian spoke.

"Let's get started." Brian paused for a moment until every attendee's gaze was on him and their pens were poised above their notepads.

Like everyone else, Jim had learned quickly that Brian maintained absolute control over the morning production meeting. Brian started the meeting when he was ready to start the meeting. No one ever assumed that it was acceptable to speak until Brian so directed. He controlled the agenda from beginning to end and gave the final approval before the meeting minutes were published.

"Rather than beginning with updates on the open issues from Friday's meeting," Brian said, "let's start with a quick summary of the factory's output and shipments on Friday and over the weekend."

That was Patricia's cue. Jim didn't hear the usual rustling of papers that often occurred when people were gathering up reports and turning to the appropriate pages. Everyone had anticipated the first topic and had their reports out and ready. Lately, output and shipments seemed to be the only focus of the production meetings.

Jim could see that Patricia was ready, too. She had likewise assumed that this would be the first topic on the agenda. Clearing her throat, she looked down at her copies of the reports and said, "Output was pretty good on Friday and over the weekend. That's especially true considering all the problems the factory has faced with the – " Putting his hand up, Brian stopped her in mid-sentence.

Bad decision! Jim thought, tensing as he waited for the inevitable. As Patricia's boss, he knew her choice of words would not only bring Brian's wrath down on her, but on himself as well.

"What do you mean that output was pretty good 'considering'?" Brian demanded. "Either the factory's output was good, and you met all of your production goals on Friday and over the weekend, or it was not good and you once again failed to successfully perform your job."

From where he was sitting, Jim could see Brian's eyes narrowing as they locked in on Patricia. He stared as if he was trying to look through her, maintaining that stare until he got the deep, red blush that appeared on her face in times of high stress and conflict.

Patricia kept her eyes fixed on the table in front of her, avoiding Brian's gaze. Her short brown hair had fallen partly across her face. Since he couldn't make eye contact with her, Brian slowly turned his head, as if to make sure that each and every person in the room saw his expression. He wanted them all to know that they had once again failed to meet his expectations.

After a few moments of silence, Brian turned his attention to Jim. "What do you have to say for yourself? Is this true?"

Jim felt sweat accumulating on his forehead as he endured the heat of Brian's attention.

"Well, the last few days in the factory have been pretty difficult," he began. "We've faced several issues. All of them have had an impact on our performance. Specifically, the new mixer on the paste dispenser isn't working as well as we thought it would."

Too late, Jim realized he had broken the unstated agreement he had made with Mary. His statement had implied that equipment problems were the biggest reason the factory was unable to meet its output goals.

"There were other—" he started to say in an attempt to deflect Brian's attack on Mary, but Brian raised his hand. It was too late now; Jim knew what would happen next. He glanced at Mary and saw her eyes fixed on him behind her wire-rimmed glasses. As the equipment maintenance manager, she would take the brunt of Brian's frustration. Several attendees shifted their gaze to her even before Brian turned to focus on his next target.

"Mary. If you'll recall, I told you during the Friday morning production meeting that I expected you to get that new mixer on the paste machine fixed. Do you remember that discussion?" Without pausing long enough even to take a breath – let alone give Mary a chance to respond—Brian continued. "I also told you that I expected you and your people to stay here until the problems were resolved. If I recall, my directive was that you do whatever it took to get the factory up and running before Monday, even if that meant that all of your people stayed here for the entire weekend. I told you to make sure that once the factory was up and running, you were to do anything that was required to keep it running. Do you remember that discussion during Friday's meeting?"

Brian stopped to catch his breath, but once again he didn't give Mary time to respond. She had begun twirling a curl of her hair around her finger as Jim had often seen her do during a confrontation.

"Obviously, that's not what you and your people did," Brian went on. "Mary, what's your problem? Did you not understand my orders, or is it that you have a problem following them? What do you have to say for yourself?" He finished his lecture in a stern whisper. His focus was totally on Mary, and his face had grown bright red.

Mary started to respond, but Brian cut her off. He wasn't done yet. Pushing back his chair, he stood up and moved toward Mary so that he was standing in front of her. She had made the strategic mistake of pushing her chair back a few inches and turning it toward the front of the room at the start of the meeting. That gave Brian the few inches he needed to position himself directly in front of her. Though Brian was barely five feet four inches tall, he still had to bend down to look at her face to face. He grabbed the arms of her chair and positioned himself so that his eyes were no more than four inches from hers. Jim cringed as he watched the spectacle.

"What do you have to say for yourself, Mary?" Brian asked again, only this time at a much higher volume. "Why didn't you follow my orders? I've had it with you! I want to see you in my office immediately after I leave this room. Be there and be ready to give me one good reason – one good reason – for not firing you today. I will not have employees who cannot or will not follow my orders!"

Brian did not move. His eyes were fixed on Mary, and he was not about to let her get away without one more tirade.

"What do you have to say for yourself? You can't even follow through on the simplest of directives. You are absolutely the worst excuse for an equipment manager I have ever seen. I don't know why I kept you in that role in the first place. Worse yet, I don't know why I've kept you on the payroll for so long. Get out! Get out of my sight, now!"

Brian jabbed a finger at the conference room door, but he didn't move back to allow Mary to leave. Jim's heart went out to her as she sat silently, her reports gripped tightly in her hands and her jaw clenched in anger. Jim was appalled, though not surprised, that Brian would treat her with such disrespect.

Mary was a very level-headed person. She would have never treated another person this way. She never criticized or attacked people in public—or in private, for that matter. She preferred instead to use calm reason, supported by facts, when communicating with people. Mary had a way of giving feedback—even difficult feedback—so that the person receiving the message was able to maintain his or her self-esteem. Jim had observed that many people almost seemed relieved after Mary had delivered a difficult message. He didn't know exactly how she did it, but employees had even thanked her for taking the time to meet and talk, to demonstrate that she really cared about them. Just the previous week, Mary had delivered a disciplinary message to an employee that had included a reduction in both pay grade and salary. That employee left the meeting and immediately started telling everyone what a great manager Mary was. She just seemed to have a gift.

That was why Jim felt that it was especially unfair how Brian was treating her, so obviously going out of his way to publicly humiliate her. Mary squirmed out of her chair, somehow avoiding having to touch Brian. She didn't even attempt to answer his questions; he obviously didn't want answers. As she slipped out the door, she made sure to give Jim a quick, angry glance to reaffirm that he had failed to meet his part of their unstated agreement.

Well, that's the end of tirade #1 for Brian, Jim thought. Based upon previous experience, he and everyone else in the room knew that at least one more person was going to be leaving the meeting early after being subjected to one of Brian's tirades. Who would it be this time?

Jim forced himself to sit still, but the others squirmed in their seats, rustling papers and glancing at one another as they braced for the rest of the meeting. A few rolled their eyes and shook their heads, as if to ask what Brian thought he had gained from this outburst. Jim even heard a few quiet whispers, but no one said a word that was loud enough for Brian to hear. That was the easiest of all methods for becoming the next victim. No one ever dared to give Brian direct feedback.

At that moment, a cloudbank dimmed the sun, and the room became much darker. Brian straightened and stood looking out the window for about 30 seconds, shaking his head and muttering under his breath. No one knew what he was saying, and no one had the courage to ask.

Jim followed Brian's gaze outside. The wall of windows overlooked a peaceful garden filled with a variety of colorful wildflowers. A slow-moving stream ran the full length of the building, meandering between birch trees and ending in a ten-foot waterfall which dropped into a pool of koi just outside the conference room. Now that the room had become deathly silent, Jim could hear the rushing sounds of the waterfall. He couldn't help thinking about the contrast between the tranquility of the garden outside versus the stress and pressure that always seemed to fill the conference room.

Finally, Brian took a deep breath and returned to his seat at the head of the table. He appeared totally composed, as if nothing of importance had occurred. His expression told them that this was just a typical Monday morning production meeting.

Chapter 2
Jim Takes a Risk

Jim could hardly believe what he had just witnessed. *Why does Brian keep doing this?* he wondered. *Demonstrate and Develop Trust and Respect – indeed!* Brian should have learned by now that he accomplished nothing by attacking people – and of all people, Mary, on top of that. Whether he realized it or not, Brian could not afford to lose her.

Mary was the last remaining person at Amber Rose with any real company experience and history. She had been with the firm almost since its beginning and was absolutely critical to the success of the factory. Mary knew more about the Amber Rose Industries factory and its products, processes, and history than the rest of the employees at the production meeting combined. If the factory was ever to get back on track and start performing to its full potential, Mary had to stay. On top of that, she was a good employee.

Brian simply could not fire Mary. In fact, Jim had to make him understand that he could not allow Mary to leave under any circumstances.

Brian took a deep breath; the meeting was ready to resume.

"Jim, you'll take over the management of all equipment and equipment maintenance in this factory," he began. "That's effective immediately. I want you to make sure the new mixer on the paste dispenser is fixed today and that the factory meets its output goals. I don't want to hear about equipment problems limiting the factory's performance. I don't want to hear about any quality issues, either. Have I made myself clear?" He glanced up from his paperwork, using eye contact to try to intimidate Jim and make sure he understood the seriousness of his demands. Jim did not look away. He had some thoughts of his own that Brian needed to hear, despite the possible consequences.

"We need to talk," Jim said, still holding eye contact with Brian. "There are some other problems that you should know about. I'd like to discuss this in private after the production meeting. Okay?"

"The decision's been made," was all Brian had to say regarding that subject. "Let's get back to the meeting. When will you have the new mixer on the paste dispenser up and running as it was advertised to do? And I'm not talking about up for only one or two hours, and then back down for adjustments and repairs." He held up his hand as Jim started to reply. "Before you answer the question, remember what just happened to Mary. You know that I expect the answer to be that it's running right now. I expect that it will stay running, too. I came to this meeting expecting that everything had been resolved over the weekend, just as I had directed Mary to do. I will not tolerate more failure. Am I making myself clear to you, Jim?"

Jim felt the frustration welling up inside him. "Brian, you know this isn't purely an equipment issue. We've got other problems that have affected the performance of that equipment, as well." He hoped Brian wouldn't see this as his attempt to avoid accepting responsibility or as a lack of support for Mary in getting the problems resolved.

"What do you mean?" Brian demanded in a whining tone. "Don't you know what to do? Don't you think you can handle this yourself? Do you need me to do your job for you again?"

Brian had started the practice of using a whining tone about two weeks after Jim joined the company. It usually came out when Jim was attempting to get Brian to look at the big picture rather than just focusing on one aspect of a problem. Jim found it very irritating. In private meetings, he'd asked Brian to stop the behavior, but his requests had apparently fallen on deaf ears.

Jim closed his eyes for a moment and decided to repeat much of the Friday report-out information for Brian. "As you will remember from the Friday morning production meeting, we've been having trouble with the viscosity of the paste ever since we made the switch over to the new mixer equipment. We've made more phone calls to the paste manufacturer than I can count. We were concerned that the paste supplier may have started sending us bad paste premix. We noticed a viscosity problem in conjunction with receipt of the last two batches of paste."

"Yes, yes, yes," Brian interrupted impatiently. "I was there for the meeting. You have a problem with the paste. Why is that my problem? You were supposed to hang around this weekend fixing it so it wouldn't have to be my problem. So why isn't it fixed?" He slammed his hand down on the table in emphasis.

"The problem," Jim continued, struggling to remain calm, "is that we haven't been able to figure out what the problem is. Both the paste premix manufacturer and our own engineering department are getting good results out of paste viscosity testing in the lab. So we eliminated the paste premix as the source of the viscosity problem. But if there isn't a paste viscosity problem, then that takes us right back to the new mixer equipment. Mary's people seem to be able to get the new equipment to work within specifications. However, after the equipment maintenance technicians turn the equipment back over to the operators, we usually need to stop running within a matter of sixty to ninety minutes. After that, the paste viscosity invariably starts drifting out of specification. It always happens somewhere in that sixty—to ninety-minute time frame."

Jim wiped sweat from his forehead as he recounted the nightmare to Brian, whose face was exhibiting ever deeper shades of red. Brian opened his mouth to speak, but Jim hurried to finish before Brian could cut him off again.

"The operators go through standard adjustments, but that doesn't get it back into safe operating specification. That means the operators need to follow procedure and shut down the equipment, purge all of the systems, reload new paste, and then contact the equipment maintenance technicians for support in bringing the equipment back up and on-line for operation. Mary and her people conduct a warm-up and then pre-flight following the procedure. Then they turn the equipment back over to the factory. It's up and running within specification at that time, so we start running again. All of the work by the operators and the equipment maintenance technicians takes about two hours.

"About sixty to ninety minutes later, we're right back where we started. Right now, for every sixty to ninety minutes we run, we are down at least one hundred twenty minutes for paste viscosity issues. Mary and her people are working this problem from the equipment side. We have both factory sustaining engineering and the semi-liquids engineering groups supporting us regarding the viscosity problem. The paste vendor has been willing to immediately test samples of paste in their lab, and has offered to send an engineer to our location if we can demonstrate that there truly is a paste premix problem. They also checked with other businesses that have received premix from this same lot, and none of them have reported a paste viscosity problem of any kind.

"The equipment manufacturer is also providing support. In addition to their call center, they're now providing a single point of contact within their engineering group to answer our questions. In fact, the equipment manufacturer's factory representative is scheduled to be here on-site within the next two weeks or so, regardless of whether we have all of our issues resolved or not."

Brian finally jumped in. "Two weeks?" he blurted. "Who can wait two more weeks? We can't wait that long. This is an equipment issue. This is inexcusable! Jim, I want to see a factory rep here, on-site, within twenty-four hours." Brian's face was flushed and his eyes bulged wider than seemed possible. He was leaning so far forward in his chair that he was almost lying on the table. Brian's secretary, who was seated immediately to his right, had to move her chair back a few inches to avoid having Brian in her lap.

Jim cleared his throat. "Uh, Brian, we aren't sure it's an equipment issue. With your permission, I'd like to stop this meeting for a few minutes. I need to gather the current status of the new mixer on the paste dispenser. Let me get the status data and the repair plans. I can also check on the equipment manufacturer and their support plans. I only need about five minutes." Jim braced himself for Brian's response.

Brian's face began to take on a purplish tinge. As he leaned across the table even further, he bumped a stack of reports and sent them cascading to the floor. "Why are you wasting my time? Why are you wasting the time of all of these people who did their preparation work and came to this meeting ready to cover all the issues in their respective areas?"

Jim flinched as Brian jabbed a finger in his face. He knew better than to interrupt Brian's tirade.

"You're the production manager. When you come to my meeting, I expect you to have all of the information about everything associated with the factory. How long will it take you to get your job down? You've been here long enough to know what I expect. When are you going to start being a contributing member of the team? When are you going to start doing your job?" Brian was panting as he finally stopped to take a breath.

Everyone knew that Brian had identified his next victim.

"Jim, I've told you never to come to this meeting unprepared. I've told you what I want you to do about the paste mix dispenser equipment. I've told you that the factory must start performing, and that I want it to start performing today. What more do I need to say?"

Brian's voice was so loud that it began to crack. He was so focused on Jim that he had forgotten about the other attendees sitting around the conference table.

"And your response is that you need time to collect more data? Get real! What kind of manager do you think you are, anyway?

What's your problem? What do I have to do to get one good, competent person into this factory?"

I am going to start doing my job right now, Jim thought as he looked around at the other employees. What was needed here was for someone to take a calculated risk, and he would be that person. He had some ideas that had been brewing since the last production meeting, and he felt he had no choice but to run with them. He had to stop Brian's tirade.

Before Brian could go any further, Jim stood and walked directly toward Brian at the front of the room. As he approached, Brian also straightened up. There they were, all five feet four inches of Brian, and all six feet three inches of Jim, not twelve inches apart. Jim couldn't help but think how comical a picture he and Brian made, staring face to face. Then he focused on the task at hand.

"Brian, when I interviewed for this job, you told me that I would have the authority to make decisions. You told me that I would be running this factory. Well, the time has come for me to use that authority. I want this meeting stopped, and I want it stopped now. I want the time to get the facts before we continue. I also want to meet with you in private. Yelling at me isn't going to change the situation in this factory one iota. There's no reason for you to make all of these employees sit here and listen to you as you yell at me.

"Darin and Patricia, I want you to leave this meeting," Jim continued, turning slightly to look at them. "I want you to go back to work in the factory. We will discuss our next steps after Brian and I are finished with our meeting. Please leave now." Jim crossed his arms as he motioned toward the conference room door with his head.

The room was so quiet that Jim thought he could have heard a pin drop. No one had ever dared question Brian before. No one had been foolish enough to interrupt him, much less take charge of one of his meetings. The others obviously didn't know what to do. For their part, Patricia and Darin looked back and forth between Jim and Brian, as if assessing which of them was the final authority. As Jim continued to motion them toward the door, they decided that he was the one to follow. They quickly gathered their paperwork and made a beeline for the door. Once their decision had been made, they were both gone within thirty seconds. Darin closed the door quietly as they left the room.

Jim knew that he had taken a risk, and one that was likely to result in his termination.

Brian was clearly caught off-guard. Since purchasing ARI, he had insisted on receiving the respect that was due the owner of a multi-million dollar firm.

"Jim, I'll meet with you right now. This won't take long." Brian was obviously irate. One by one, the others stood up, gathered their paperwork, and followed Darin and Patricia out of the conference room. From the furtive glances they gave him, Jim could see that they expected a new production manager to be hired within the next few days, along with the new equipment maintenance manager. They figured that Jim's foolish actions would cost him his job; he hoped to prove them wrong.

After the last person had left the room, Jim closed the door and turned back to Brian, whose fists were clenched in rage.

"How dare you show me that kind of disrespect!" Brian erupted. "Even more, how dare you do it in front of my employees! I own this company, and no one is going to get away with treating me this way. Jim, that includes you. I will not stand for it! Clean out your desk. Pack up your belongings. You are history to this company. And don't bother to ask me for a reference. You won't like what you hear." Brian smoothed his tie and headed for the door.

"Brian, stop!" Jim said. "I apologize for what just happened. But please sit down and listen to me. You hired me to help you get your factory performing. You were losing customers due to missed delivery dates and product quality issues long before I got here. Why won't you let me do my job? Why won't you let me run the factory for you?"

"Let you run the factory? What do think I've been—"

This time Jim held up his hand to quiet Brian. "Please let me finish. If you want me to leave, fine. But if you want me to help pull your team together and start getting results from the factory, then you need to take a step back and really allow me to do my job. You need to allow me to make the decisions that are required to get the right results, and people need to see that you support those decisions. You also need to start treating people with a little respect. Otherwise, you're going to lose the last few loyal employees that have remained with you." Jim took a deep breath. He hoped Brian would take the time to think before he responded.

Brian, obviously startled by Jim's directness, stared at him without moving closer to the door.

"Working together, Mary and I can get your factory back on track," Jim continued. "In fact, if we stay, Mary and I will have a complete action plan developed and ready for you to review this afternoon. We'll have everything positioned to begin immediately after we receive your approval."

For once, Brian seemed to be at a loss for words. He broke eye contact and looked down at the polished conference table, rubbing his hand along the surface. Jim tried to evaluate whether he had convinced Brian to accept his proposal. The silence could mean that Brian was preparing to erupt again or, perhaps, that he was actually considering what Jim had said. Although his stomach was in knots, Jim decided to make one last plea.

"If you don't like the plan, or the results that I'm willing to commit to, then I'll agree with you. You won't need to fire me; I'll willingly leave. It seems to me that you have nothing to lose and everything to gain by hearing the plan we present. Don't you agree?"

Some of the anger seemed to drain out of Brian's face. He fell into his chair, looking very tired.

"You've made some good points," he conceded grudgingly. "While I don't approve of your approach, it's true that I have nothing to lose by giving you a second chance. I hired you because you're a team player and you know manufacturing. The factory is…" He paused and seemed to revise his word choice. "Production here could possibly benefit from some new ideas. I'll give you and Mary until the end of the day to have a complete action plan that has this factory performing as committed. I'll talk to Mary and see if we can come to an agreement."

Jim released a pent-up breath in relief. He sensed that Brian was worried about Mary's reaction to Jim's idea, in light of his earlier tirade. It occurred to Jim that Brian truly was desperate. Considering the snowballing problems the factory was facing, it wasn't just Jim whose future was in jeopardy, but Brian and the entire company. He had no doubt that the stress was also finding its way into Brian's reactions to problems with the factory. Underneath it all, maybe Brian wasn't as bad as he often came across to his employees.

Brian stood, gathered his paperwork, and moved past Jim to the door of the conference room. He didn't look at Jim or wait for any kind of acknowledgement from him. Then, at the doorway, he paused and turned.

"And Jim, you had better bring a good action plan to the meeting; one that works," he said, his voice hardening again. "You will not be getting another chance from me." With that he left, pulling the door shut behind him.

Jim heaved a sigh and sat down, exhausted. As he straightened his own stack of paperwork, he couldn't help but wonder what he had started. Would Mary even consider staying after the way Brian had treated her during the meeting? She had told Jim that if Brian ever attacked her again in public, she would tender her resignation on the spot, and nothing would change her mind. Jim also knew that several competitors had been aggressively recruiting her during the past two to three weeks.

If Mary did stay, was there even enough time to develop the right plan to address the factory's issues? Could they do it in less than a day? If an action plan was developed and presented, would Brian approve? If Brian did approve the action plan, would the workforce buy in and work to the changes required by the plan? If everything fell into place perfectly, would Brian give them enough time to improve performance to the point where the factory was meeting its production goals? Jim knew the questions would just keep coming.

Mary's decision was what mattered most right now. After all, Jim had in essence given her the power to determine whether he was even remaining as an ARI employee. Jim didn't have the offers from competitors that Mary obviously had in place. For his family's sake, he hoped that she would decide to stay for at least a little while longer.

No matter the outcome, Jim knew that he had better update and polish his resume. He would also make some subtle job contacts.

Jim decided to proceed immediately to the factory and then find Mary. An action plan for the future wouldn't matter if he didn't get the factory back on track today. He needed to make sure that the right focus was being placed on resolving both the problems with the new mixer on the paste dispenser and the paste pre-mix viscosity issues. There were also other issues that they had not even discussed during the production meeting.

As he entered the factory, Jim began searching for one of the production supervisors. He would get a thorough update and then make sure that the right actions were under way.

Jim quickly located Patricia and Pedro, one of the equipment maintenance supervisors. He spent fifteen minutes reviewing the current status of the key equipment, as well as the plans for the day. He also reviewed the information that Patricia and Pedro provided about output and quality for the current shift.

On the way back to his office, Jim decided to stop by the front lobby to make sure that Mary had remained in the building after the morning meeting disaster.

Chapter 3
Brian's Meeting with Mary

As Mary waited in Brian's office for her soon-to-be ex-boss to arrive, she couldn't help but think about all the years she had spent with Amber Rose Industries. She had been the tenth employee hired. She was also the first non-engineer employee. She had actually started working as the first operator in the former owner's garage.

While the story about the company's humble beginnings impressed those who were not there when it happened, Mary knew exactly how difficult starting the business had been. Oh, how she remembered those cold winter days spent working without adequate heat, and those hot summer days working without air conditioning. Mary remembered the pressures of not having everything necessary to build products because of missed payments to vendors. She remembered the pride of being the first person to build products and the first to see those products that she had built actually work. She remembered the closeness and teamwork she had felt working side-by-side with the engineers, developing and debugging products as they were producing them to fill orders for delivery. It was amazing that the business had even survived, much less thrived. One of the things Mary missed the most about those start-up days was that every employee was able to maintain a good sense of humor no matter what the challenge.

After three years, Mary had been promoted from her operator position. She became the first factory equipment maintenance technician the day she had obtained her technical associate's degree from the local community college. She had been very proud of that promotion and held the equipment maintenance technician position for several years.

Mary had continued her education and was offered an engineering position upon obtaining her bachelor's degree. The engineering position didn't last long, however. While Mary had enjoyed the challenges associated with her new position, she really missed the manufacturing environment too much to stay away. She requested a move back to the factory and became the company's first full-time factory-sustaining engineer.

Over time, Mary's role changed from sustaining engineer to sustaining engineering manager, and she began to supervise a small team of factory-focused sustaining engineers. During the past year, Mary had assumed the role of factory equipment-engineering manager in addition to her factory sustaining engineering manager duties. In that expanded role, Mary was responsible for the management of all of the factory's equipment. She also managed four equipment maintenance supervisors, who had thirteen equipment maintenance technicians reporting to them. Mary enjoyed the added management responsibility. She felt that she had been extremely successful in fulfilling her duties. She was proud of her many accomplishments during her employment with ARI, and proud of the team that she had developed.

As Mary thought about the ARI of today, it was difficult not to be sad about the changes that had taken place. Rather than being a team that tackled problems and challenges head-on as in the past, today's approach seemed to be to blame people who were working as hard as they possibly could whenever a problem appeared – and these were the people who wanted to do the right thing. They really wanted to see Amber Rose succeed.

What a shame to be leaving ARI after all these years, she thought. Amber Rose was like her second home.

Since Brian Jones had purchased Amber Rose Industries, nothing had been the same. She thought back to all the people who had left the company already. Jim James was the third production manager to be hired in six months, and Pat Peters was the fourth quality manager in that same period. Both of the production supervisors, Patricia and Darin, had been with ARI for less than four months. Every supervisor now working for Mary had been hired since Brian Jones had purchased ARI.

Sure, they had never had so much business, but no one had any authority to make decisions. Everything, including purchases, had to be approved by Brian. On one hand, he wanted to increase output. On the other hand, he would delay spending on equipment maintenance parts, tools, and supplies or staff training by taking up to four weeks to review a request to spend money. Even then, he often dismissed the request as unnecessary or too expensive. It was always the same thing.

Worse yet, Brian showed no respect for his employees. He thought nothing of making a public spectacle of people. He would stop them in the hallway, in the factory, or in a meeting and begin his barrage. Yet Brian had appeared to be a very reasonable and congenial man when he had first purchased Amber Rose Industries. What had made him change?

Mary couldn't believe that she had actually been excited about Brian's arrival. When Mr. Ross had introduced Brian to all of the managers as a part of the sales transaction, Brian had talked about how impressed he was with the success of Amber Rose Industries and had acknowledged the credit that Mr. Ross had given to all of the managers for making it a success. Brian had indicated that he wanted every manager to remain and that he looked forward to the partnership they would all have in growing ARI to higher levels of success.

When he had first arrived, Brian had been eager to focus on the customer service and marketing sides of the business. He had pretty much left the factory to Mary and Ben Price, the production manager at that time. Then, as the factory had difficulty bringing in the new equipment and products that had been added, Brian had started to change. He didn't understand the lead-time that was required to install and qualify new equipment, or to bring a new product or process up to full production rates. He didn't understand the learning curves that operators went through when new equipment, products, and processes were added. He insisted on immediate, full-scale output regardless of the issues they faced. He would get angrier and angrier when the factory failed to start a new product, process, or piece of equipment at 100% output. One by one, the entire management team that he had said he wanted to keep had left Amber Rose. Brian had changed, and Mary was convinced that he was not going to change back.

Mary had only one choice, and that choice was simple: it was time to leave Amber Rose Industries. She had been interviewing with a competitor, and they had made a very nice formal offer. Even though she hated leaving the company where her career had started and grown, and even though she hated leaving those few friends who were still with the company, today would be the day that Mary resigned from ARI. Mary would accept the position with their competitor today.

Mary's thoughts were interrupted as Brian strode into his office. She refused to meet his eyes; she would not give him the satisfaction of intimidating her one more time. Gripping her letter of resignation tightly, she noticed that her hand was shaking. She forced herself to take a deep breath.

Before sitting down at his desk, Brian paused and returned to his office doorway. Mary could overhear him instructing the secretary to hold all calls before he closed the door. Probably he didn't want anyone interrupting the final tirade he had planned for her.

Sitting down at his desk, Brian cleared his throat but didn't immediately speak. When Mary finally looked up, she thought Brian seemed unusually nervous. For a moment he busied himself with loosening his tie and straightening the papers on his desk. Mary hoped he was regretting his decision to humiliate her the way he had —not that it would change her decision.

He cleared his throat again and said, "Mary, I think we need to talk about what happened after you left the morning production meeting."

Mary shook her head. "I don't care what happened after I left the meeting. All I care about is that you accept my two weeks notice of termination." She gestured at the folded paper in her hand as she placed it on top of Brian's desk and slid it a few inches in his direction. "I'm going to seek employment with a company where I can feel that I'm valued, where I can make contributions that will be recognized and valued." Mary's voice got louder with each word. The more she spoke, the angrier the whole experience made her feel. "Brian, I have been one of your most loyal employees since you purchased ARI, yet that loyalty has meant nothing to you. I really don't think we have anything to talk about. This is my formal letter of resignation." She pushed the paper further in Brian's direction as she prepared to stand and leave his office.

"Mary—please hold onto that letter of resignation for a minute. Won't you please give me a minute to respond?" Brian held up his hand in a beseeching manner. "I apologize for the way you feel. You are valued and respected, especially by Jim. Jim says he's quitting if you leave. To be honest, I can't afford to lose one of you, much less both of you. Jim has asked that I allow the two of you to develop an action plan that will get the factory back on track. You're a key person in the development and execution of any such plan. Jim feels that we can't be successful in meeting delivery and quality goals without you. Frankly, I agree with him completely."

Mary had never seen a look of fear on Brian's face before. He was clearly anxious about her response, afraid that she really would be leaving the company. Why had his behavior changed so much? Only an hour earlier, he had been asking her to explain how she brought any value to Amber Rose. He had threatened to fire her. Now, when she was ready to resign, Brian was practically begging her to stay.

What had happened at the production meeting after Mary had left? Why was Brian so desperate all of a sudden?

Mary sat back in her chair. "What plan are you talking about?" she asked warily.

"I don't know. The factory is in trouble. ARI is in big trouble. We need to do something to get the factory back on track." He flicked his hand nervously. "Please, just meet with Jim. All I know is that he told me the two of you would be handing me a plan sometime later this afternoon. Mary, I need you to stay with ARI. Please, will you at least meet with Jim?"

In her heart, Mary really wanted to remain with ARI. Even now, however, despite his desperation, Brian was still having trouble acknowledging that he valued and respected Mary for her contributions. He was basically saying that it was Jim who valued her. Could she believe that Brian really felt they would not be successful without her?

She stared at the top of Brian's desk for at least two minutes as she contemplated her options. Brian continued to fidget in his seat while he waited. Finally, she decided that she could take the time to see what this was all about.

"I guess I don't have anything to lose by meeting with Jim," she conceded. "I'll meet with him before I hand this letter of resignation over to you." Mary pulled the folded letter back into her hand as she stood up to leave. "I don't think there's much Jim can say that could change my mind at this point. I'll get back to you with my decision within the hour."

With that, Mary was out the door.

Brian rubbed a hand over his face and leaned back in his executive office chair. He couldn't believe how his world was crashing down around him. He had purchased the business only last spring. It had seemed like such a sure winner, yet today there was no money left to pay the bills.

The previous owner had started Amber Rose Industries in his garage only eight years earlier. When Brian bought the business, it was a highly profitable, multimillion-dollar enterprise. There was also a newly signed contract that would double sales revenue within the next ninety days.

Brian had been a marketing executive with a competitor for many years, and he had seen the chance to grow the business even further. But the factory was turning out to be one headache after another. Orders were not being delivered on time, and customers were upset about quality problems. Orders were decreasing at an alarming rate, which was particularly embarrassing since Brian's specialty was sales. There was even talk that the new contract would be cancelled due to the quality issues and poor delivery performance. The factory had become the source of many sleepless nights for Brian, and it would soon be the cause of the ARI's demise. The stress and lack of sleep wasn't helping the way he dealt with the problems, either.

Brian was relieved beyond words that Mary had accepted his plea to speak with Jim. Perhaps she would stay, after all. After that surprising meeting with Jim, he had felt it would be just his luck to have Mary leave the building or refuse to meet with him. He had let his frustration spiral out of control one too many times, and now those mistakes might come back to haunt him when he needed Mary most. How had it come down to this?

Thinking over Jim's proposal, Brian remembered why he had hired the young man. He was an intelligent risk-taker, yet he always considered the pros and cons before taking a stand. When Jim did make a commitment, he had always delivered.

Jim must have sensed the precarious position that the company was in. He must have already known that ARI was close to bankruptcy. What other reason would have motivated him to make such a career-ending move?

Brian hoped that Jim did have the answer to getting the factory on track and performing. Maybe he had ideas that Brian hadn't seen or heard before. He hated to admit it, but Jim was right: Brian had been trying to run the factory, and he needed to allow Jim to start running it instead. Jim was also right in asking what Brian had to lose. He was in desperate straits.

Brian put his thoughts about the factory out of his head and decided to call the bank to see if they had made a decision on extending his line of credit. He needed them to say yes.

Chapter 4

The Planning Begins

Jim didn't have to look very hard to find Mary. He was hurrying to the lobby when he almost ran into her just down the hallway from Brian's office. He eyed her carefully, trying to gauge her feelings after meeting with Brian.

"What's this about a plan?" she asked in a low voice. "Brian says we're creating a plan. What's he talking about?"

Mary didn't appear to be in the mood that he had hoped. Rather than being excited about the opportunity to partner with Jim in the development, implementation, and execution of an action plan to improve the factory's performance, Mary seemed upset.

Jim had seen the look before. It was the same look he had seen on the faces of the angrier employees who had recently left ARI. Some of those employees had stopped by Jim's desk to say goodbye, and Jim hadn't been able to overlook the anger and frustration he had seen on their faces. It was the look of an employee who had given up on being able to change the working conditions that surrounded them. They had decided to move on to other opportunities. For some, that meant leaving the only employer they had ever known. For others, it had meant uprooting their families as a consequence of accepting another position. For many it had meant leaving family and friends in search of another job. Jim would never forget that look.

He gently took Mary's elbow and led her down the hall, away from Brian's office. "Mary, let's go into a conference room. I'll be happy to answer your questions. I'll need only a few minutes to tell you what I have in mind about the plan."

They stepped into the first unoccupied conference room they found. Conference Room A – if you could call it a conference room – was approximately six feet wide and eight feet long. It had been an architect's answer for what to do with a small corner directly off the main entryway lobby, a leftover space that originally had no defined use. The space would have made an adequate broom closet.

Jim and Mary sat down at the small round table positioned in the center of those forty-eight square feet. Jim had previously endured a few brief meetings in this room and remembered the small marker board on one wall and the inadequate yellow light from the overhead fixture. There were no windows and no phone. All of the plumbing for the factory went through the east wall of the conference room, and the muted roar of large air compressors came from the room next door. In all, the environment did not foster creative thought. In fact, people laughed when they were assigned CR-A for meetings, knowing the meeting would be virtually pointless.

In that dreary, cramped CR-A environment, Jim began to explain the details of his plan. He stayed focused on the highlights, the results that he hoped to achieve, and the way he hoped to achieve them.

As he was explaining the details, Jim couldn't help but wonder if Mary was okay. Worry lines marked her forehead, and she kept nervously biting her lip. He couldn't tell whether she was even listening. Was she going to follow through on her decision to leave if Brian ever embarrassed her again in public – which he certainly had done today? Would she even consider staying as a co-owner of the plan? Jim had hoped that she would share his vision, but she seemed wary.

"Mary, what do you think so far? Are you willing to work with me on this? I know you must be upset about what happened today."

,

41

Mary slumped back in her chair. "I had really planned on leaving Amber Rose this morning. It was very hard for me to make this decision. I don't want to go through any more of this. After making my decision and communicating it to Brian, I suddenly found out that you committed me to co-own the creation and execution of a recovery action plan for the factory. You're asking me to do more work for Amber Rose!" She shook her head despondently. "I just don't know if I have the power in me to continue. I know that I won't accept being treated like that ever again in public or in private by Brian. I deserve more. Besides, I'm concerned that your plan is too late. All you're doing is delaying the inevitable."

Mary was more animated than Jim had ever seen her. She seemed relieved to get her thoughts and emotions out on the table. Jim felt how deeply she had been hurt by Brian's treatment during the past months. He knew that he was asking a lot of her. He also knew that he needed her expertise and support if his plan had any chance of succeeding in time to meet his commitments to Brian.

"Mary, I know we can do this together." Jim leaned toward her, raising his voice to be heard over the noise of the air compressors as they started up next door. "We're a team. If Brian will give us the leeway, we can make it work. Please invest one day with me in planning the right actions to take. After all these years of working for ARI, how about it? I don't think you have anything to lose except one day of your time. Potentially, you have everything to gain, and ARI has everything to gain as well. With the plan that we develop today, we'll be on our way to having a factory that's meeting its goals and performing to expectations. You can be a part of making that happen. Isn't it worth a day of your time to see the details?"

He paused expectantly, but he could see that she was still hesitant.

"You can decide whether you want to help make the action plan a reality after you've seen what we've developed and how Brian reacts to it. If you don't think the plan will turn the factory's performance around, or if you don't like what Brian has to say during the presentation, you can still tender your resignation. Please? What do you think?"

The room was silent as Mary rethought it over. She stared at the door as she took what seemed like an eternity to make her decision. Then she sighed.

"All right," she said finally, nodding her head slightly. "I'll help you develop the plan. But I'm not committing to stay beyond that. I want to see how Brian responds to the plan before I commit to more than one day." Mary had been looking at the table as she spoke. Now she looked up, and her eyes locked on Jim's. "Let's get started. Where do we go from here?"

No one could have ever imagined that CR-A would be the location where the action plan to save the ARI factory got its start. This action plan would define the first steps in moving the Amber Rose Industries factory toward becoming a world-class manufacturing facility.

"For starters, we've both been taking notes during the daily production meetings," Jim began. "Let's use those notes as the basis for defining the problem statement. We also have the notes we've taken during our own daily meetings and lunches together and whenever employees have given us feedback about their concerns. Those will provide more data to help develop and validate the problem statement. I think most of the issues that are causing the factory to under-perform are documented in those notes. We may even have many of the solutions identified, as well.

"What we haven't done is identify exactly what the problems are. We haven't put them into a comprehensive action plan, and we haven't quantified the potential gains. We haven't taken the time to see if we have the problem well defined, and if we have the right action plan to achieve a complete solution."

As Mary listened, it was as if a cloud lifted from her face. She sat up straighter and looked Jim in the eye. "You're right. I wish we hadn't waited until now to do this."

Lately, Jim and Mary had been talking about some of the ideas they had hoped to implement. They had even talked about the improvements in performance that they thought they could achieve. But until now they hadn't been able to aggressively pursue those improvements. Jim knew Mary didn't hide from problems; she faced them head-on and achieved results. Now she seemed ready to face the factory's problems and help fix them.

"Will we be able to do all the planning work in one day?" she asked. "Do you really think we'll be ready for Brian this afternoon?"

Jim smiled and began to relax. He realized that Mary was truly willing to stay and partner for the success of the factory after all.

"Mary, I know you and I can create a sound plan with the help of our supervisors. Our teams can help make that plan work."

"Okay," Mary responded. "But I need about thirty minutes to make sure the right priorities are being worked in the factory and to pull my notes together. I also need to let Brian know that I'll be holding onto my letter of resignation for at least a little while longer."

"Let's meet back here in thirty minutes," said Jim. "I need to spend some time with Patricia and Darin to make sure they're working the right issues in the factory as well. I spent a few minutes in the factory while you were meeting with Brian, and I'm sure that everyone left the morning production meeting feeling very confused. Since we'll need the supervisors to spend the afternoon working on the plan with us, I want to make sure they've gotten everything started in the factory and that they'll take the time to get their notes and data assembled before we start this afternoon. I suggest that you do the same with your equipment maintenance supervisors."

Mary nodded in agreement. She and Jim walked to the factory floor together and then parted ways to meet with the supervisors who worked under them.

After getting their factory updates and providing direction on actions to take, Jim met with each of the supervisors individually. During those brief discussions, he explained the strategy that he and Mary planned to use in developing the recovery action plan. He then asked them to be prepared for the afternoon meeting.

Returning to his desk, Jim collected his notes from the daily production meetings, weekly supervisor meetings, and employee feedback. Individually, both he and Mary had been collecting other supporting information over the past several weeks. He included any information that he thought might be important in the development of a sound recovery action plan. After a short rest in the break room and a much-needed cup of coffee, he headed back to CR-A.

After Mary finished her own preparation for the action-planning meeting with Jim, she sat behind her desk and found herself thinking about Jim and his performance at Amber Rose. She had developed a deep respect for Jim – a respect that he had earned. Sure, Mary was initially impressed with both Jim's manufacturing management experience and the successes that he had already achieved. She was also initially impressed with Jim's engineering degree, which had been followed so quickly by an Ivy League MBA. But what mattered most to Mary was that Jim had earned her respect. He had shown himself to be a knowledgeable, trustworthy, and hardworking manager. He knew the mechanics of his job well.

Mary truly felt that Jim would have made a major positive impact on the factory by now if Brian had only given him the opportunity to take control and implement some of the changes that he had suggested during meetings and discussions. Mary didn't understand why Jim had chosen to remain with ARI under these working conditions. Surely he would have had his choice of many companies if those companies had known that he was seeking employment. All Jim would tell Mary when she asked him about this was that he had signed on with Amber Rose for the long-term and that he was committed to making the factory a success.

Glancing at her watch, Mary forced herself to get up and perform the task that she most hated. She spoke with Brian's secretary, who then escorted Mary into his office. Brian was still seated at his desk, looking as if he had not moved since their earlier meeting. He seemed to be anxiously awaiting Mary's response.

Standing behind one of the visitor chairs, she cleared her throat and said, "Based on my meeting with Jim, I've decided to stay with Amber Rose for at least the rest of the day. I understand what Jim intends to do, and I've agreed to help him develop a factory performance recovery action plan."

A look of relief came over Brian. "I'm glad to hear that. I guess I'll see you at the action plan presentation?"

"Yes, and following the meeting I'll let you know whether you'll still be receiving my resignation."

Brian nodded. "I understand."

Without another word, Mary turned and left Brian's office. The entire discussion had taken less than sixty seconds.

When she returned to her office to retrieve the box of paperwork she was bringing to the conference room, she glanced at the now crumpled letter of resignation on her desk. She made a mental note to print a new copy of the letter before she presented it to Brian – assuming that she did, indeed, present it to him.

Chapter 5
Identifying the Issues

The plan development meeting started promptly at 10:45 a.m., as planned. When Jim arrived, he found Mary neatly sorting the information she had brought to the meeting in a cardboard box. Having been unable to find a box for his own use, Jim hurried to the table balancing a disorganized pile of folders and papers about eighteen inches thick. He barely made it to the table before the papers began to slide in all directions. Sighing, he picked them up from the floor and the chair and proceeded to place them into a single pile.

As they both sat down, Jim looked at what was before them and guessed that to an outsider, the scene would have been comical. In front of each of them was an overwhelmingly huge pile of papers. To Jim, however, the paperwork meant that business was about to start.

"So, where do we start?" asked Mary..

She and Jim discussed some options for getting through all the notes piled on the table, and finally agreed that the limited amount of available time forced them to spend no more than a total of three hours identifying the key issues their plan needed to address.

The first two hours would be spent summarizing the information they had previously discussed onto flip charts, in addition to anything else of importance from the other paperwork. Then they would spend no more than 30 minutes placing common ideas and topics together under specific titles. Finally, they would prioritize the titles based on the number and significance of issues. They agreed to a rating criterion and started the process.

It was an intense and grueling three hours. Jim's stomach was growling and his head aching by the time they were finished. They had identified and titled five key categories of issues. Each included many specific examples. In reviewing the pages of flip charts before them, Mary and Jim agreed that they had at least twenty examples for every category they had identified. They consolidated those twenty examples down to three or four representative examples.

The selected categories and their examples would first be presented to the supervisors as grounding information for their action-planning meeting. Later, Jim and Mary would use those same examples during their presentation to Brian.

Reviewing their notes a final time, Mary and Jim were confident that they had selected categories that were truly key causes for current factory performance levels. They agreed that if all of these categories were adequately addressed, there would be a significant improvement in the factory's level of performance, and it would be able to meet current production goals.

Issue #1—Communication

Lack of communication, wrong communication, and misunderstood communication were all having negative effects on the results employees achieved. Mary and Jim were shocked by the impact to the factory that poor communication was having.

Examples:
1) On September 9, the laser/cut machine had been left idle for over four hours.

Background: At the end of the shift on September 8, Tom, the equipment maintenance technician for the laser/cut machine, had contacted one of the equipment operators. Tom had instructed the operator not to perform an equipment pre-flight and not to start running the equipment on the morning of the ninth. The plan was for Tom to perform preventative maintenance at the start of the shift. Since an equipment pre-flight was part of the preventative maintenance process, Tom would perform the pre-flight when he was done with the preventative maintenance.

On September 9, Tom had called his supervisor to report that he had a family emergency and would not be able to report to work that day. Tom, who was obviously distraught, failed to mention anything about the planned maintenance. Since no one but Tom and the equipment operator had been aware of the plan to perform the maintenance, and since the operator had not been told that Tom would not be coming to work, the equipment sat idle for the first four hours of the shift. If it had not been for the alert questioning of another operator, the equipment might have been left down for the entire shift.

There was only one laser/cut machine in the Amber Rose factory. That machine was typically required to run every minute of every shift to keep up with the rest of the factory. It was expected that there would be lost output during all scheduled maintenance. However, failing to perform preventative maintenance on schedule had also proven to be extremely costly to the factory. Those four hours of downtime on September 9 had reduced the entire factory's output by 50% for the day.

2) On September 18, the laser/cut machine vendor came into the factory unexpectedly and asked the operator if he could use the machine for a one-hour sales demonstration to a potential new customer.

Background: When the vendor arrived, the operator looked for either Darin or Patricia. Neither could be located anywhere in the factory. As it turned out, Darin was at his desk reading and responding to e-mail. He assumed that Patricia would follow her usual routine and remain in the factory for the balance of the morning. On this particular morning, however, Patricia had been asked to join the engineering team in a preview of the next generation Robotic Parts Mover (RPM). Engineering was excited about the advances that had been made. These advances included the addition of a safety sensor to eliminate parts damage, a 2x increase in the speed of movement, a breakthrough in cleanliness due to a new process that sealed all RPM moving parts, and the elimination of all on-site maintenance through the addition of a 100,000-hour vendor exchange policy.

Since the laser/cut machine vendor had been supportive of requests to fix issues associated with the machine, and since the operator felt that she had been forced to make the decision due to the absence of a supervisor, she turned the laser/cut machine over to the vendor. During the demonstration, in an attempt to demonstrate that the laser/cut machine could exceed all specified parameters of operation, the vendor broke the machine. He was attempting to cut at an angle of 145 degrees, even though the head rotation stop was placed at 120 degrees. The vendor inadvertently broke the rotator/ stop mechanism during that portion of the demonstration.

There was no backup rotator/stop mechanism in the equipment spare parts storage area. After several hours of calling the factory, parts distributors, and other laser/cut equipment users, the vendor located a replacement rotator/stop mechanism. It was to be overnight expressed to the local airport. The vendor would be at the airport to meet the flight and would personally hand-carry it to the factory. A vendor's factory technician flew in to install the new part and re-qualify the equipment. This was all done at no charge to Amber Rose Industries, of course.

The replacement rotator/stop mechanism was inadvertently shipped to a town in Rhode Island by the same name, rather than to Amber Rose's hometown. After tracking down the error and rebooking the shipment, another day was lost. The new rotator/stop mechanism was finally received, qualified, installed, and preflighted by noon on September 20. Production time lost: nineteen hours. As with example number one, this directly impacted total factory output by nineteen hours.

3) There were many specific examples of poor management communication. Jim and Mary picked out three or four specific examples to underscore the importance of this line item.

3a) Many of the factory's personnel voiced concerns about not knowing how well the factory was performing.

Background: Having not received any specific communication from management, employees cited various rumors when asked about the factory's performance. The last time they had seen Brian was about three months earlier, when he had told everyone how well the company was doing. He had been in the midst of introducing one of the new production managers. Most thought it had been about two production managers ago.

While many acknowledged that Jim and Mary had provided some information, most said they didn't fully grasp what Jim and Mary were talking about. When describing performance, Jim and Mary used words and phrases like "Okay," "It's going well," or "We need to keep our focus," which implied that goals were being met.

Since they didn't know for sure, each employee who was questioned indicated that he or she thought everything was "Okay, or someone would have told us." All noted that in general, the people upstairs (Management and Engineering) appeared to be in a "bad mood." In all cases, these employees did not know that the factory was not meeting output goals, which was negatively affecting customers. In all cases, these employees did not know that the factory had a variety of product quality issues, which were also affecting their customers.

3b) Several different people complained because they did not know that Jim's predecessor had even left the company.

Background: Brian had discontinued the practice of personally introducing new managers, and since there was no memo regarding the change, employees were surprised. Many had genuinely liked Jim's predecessor and would have wanted to say goodbye had they known that she was leaving. The operators said they had found out about the change when they saw Jim and found out that he was the new production manager.

Issue #2—Policies, Procedures, Guidelines, and Expectations

The use of different interpretations and enforcement created both confusion and morale issues within the workforce. Many employees felt that they were being treated unfairly. They could not understand why employees working in the same factory on the same shift, with the same policies and guidelines in place, should be treated with favoritism.

Again, there were many examples of breakdowns in the administration of company policies, guidelines, and expectations.

1a) Attendance Guidelines: Absenteeism
Background: Darin and Patricia had discussed, and were in total agreement about, the treatment of absenteeism. Company policy provided every employee with a specific number of paid absence hours. Absence hours accrued based on the number of hours an employee actually worked. Employees who exceeded the hours that were in their absence hours account were subject to discipline. Both supervisors consistently followed the disciplinary guidelines when an employee exceeded the absence hours policy.

Mary's equipment maintenance technicians were subject to the same policy. However, Mary's supervisors did not follow the documented disciplinary guidelines when one of the equipment maintenance technicians exceeded the absence hours guideline. The equipment maintenance supervisors felt that the policy was too strict. They were consistent in their decision not to adhere to the disciplinary guideline.

The equipment maintenance technicians had shared this with most of the factory operators who were being disciplined. The operators, in turn, had complained to Patricia and Darin, as well as to Jim and Mary about this discrepancy in treatment.

Patricia and Darin had attempted to address this discrepancy with Mary's supervisors, but they were told that the equipment maintenance supervisors had no intention of changing. Instead, the equipment maintenance supervisors had directed Patricia and Darin to change their adherence to the guideline. Further, the equipment maintenance supervisors told Patricia and Darin that they felt that their equipment maintenance technicians should be treated "better" than the operators since they were more important to the long-term success of Amber Rose Industries.

1b) Attendance Guidelines: Tardiness

Background: Darin and Patricia had different interpretations of the guidelines associated with exactly where an employee should physically be located at the start of each work period. In conjunction with that disconnect, they also disagreed on exactly what constituted employee tardiness to work. The guideline in question stated that employees were expected to be at their designated workstations when the work period started.

Patricia took a more liberal approach, allowing employees to be as much as five minutes late in reporting to their designated work stations as long as they were in the building at the start of the work period.

Darin, on the other hand, strictly interpreted the guideline to mean that being in the building was not good enough. He expected employees to be at their assigned workstations in the factory. His only exception was if he had personally assigned an employee to be at some other specific location. Training in a classroom, for example, met Darin's criteria. Since Darin and Patricia supervised employees who worked side-by-side in the factory, there had been many complaints to Jim from Darin's people about the unfair treatment that he gave them. Patricia's employees acknowledged that there was a difference in treatment, but were less inclined to bring it up as an issue. They were satisfied with the way Patricia treated them.

2) Overtime Sign-Up Process

Background: In an attempt to create a more positive work environment, one of Jim's predecessors had developed a process which allowed those operators who wished to work overtime to place their names on a sign-up list. When extra help was required, the supervisors would use that list to call in personnel to cover the overtime need.

The process called for contacting the first person on the list. If that person wished to work, he or she got to work. If #1 on the list did not wish to work, then the supervisor would call #2 on the list. The supervisor would continue numerically through the employee list until someone accepted the overtime work.

The process called for #1 to go to the bottom of the list once that employee was contacted. The same process was followed with all subsequent employees who were contacted. As time passed, the theory was that this process allowed every employee who wished to work overtime to receive an equal opportunity to do so.

If employees wished to withdraw their names from consideration for overtime, they had access to the list and could simply remove their names.

Darin again remained firm in his adherence to the process. Patricia, on the other hand, had found that there were some workers whom she preferred to call for overtime. She had gotten into the practice of using three or four specific employees on a routine basis to cover all of her overtime needs. In Patricia's view, these particular employees worked harder and required less of her time to manage. This practice caused resentment among those who had signed up for overtime but were never called by Patricia.

Several employees had been very vocal in their protests regarding this practice. They had complained to Patricia, then to Darin, and finally to Jim.

3) Not Following Defined Process

Background: On September 27, one of the press engineers added the requirement that a new visual inspection temporarily be conducted at the flying backlash machine. This was to check the quality of the holes at location 3-Y. The engineer had made some pressure changes as part of an experiment, and he wanted to make sure that the outgoing product met all quality specifications. This inspection added approximately fifteen seconds per assembly to the total process time.

The automatic reset button tripped at twenty-nine seconds, allowing only five seconds of extra time. As a result of the added visual inspection, two equipment maintenance technicians were required to spend virtually the entire shift at the flying backlash machines to push the automatic reset after every pre-assembly was completed through the new visual inspection.

This experiment significantly decreased output for the ten shifts that it was in place. It also left equipment down and awaiting attention from the remaining equipment maintenance technicians on the shifts, which further reduced the total factory output for those shifts.

When confronted about the huge impact that this temporary visual inspection was having on meeting customer deliveries, the engineer who was responsible for the change informed Mary. The engineer had not been aware of the extra equipment resets that his inspection would cause when he decided to make the pressure adjustments that drove the need for the inspection. He thought it was a straightforward request and had not followed the normal approval process. That approval process would have required the engineer to first gain both process engineering and factory engineering approvals to make changes to the process flow.

The engineer had not been to the factory since making the modification, as critical issues with a new product had arisen. He had expected that if problems arose, someone would just come and get him so that he could help fix the problem.

While the engineer had not followed the approval process, Mary was also concerned when she heard that no factory personnel had made an attempt to contact the engineer. Certainly there were enough impacts to factory performance to warrant someone taking the initiative to immediately contact the engineer. She decided to further investigate the circumstances surrounding the incident.

Mary interviewed all of the equipment maintenance technicians who had been required to complete the manual resets. She also interviewed all of the flying backlash operators. They all felt that for an inspection to be implemented, there must have been a quality issue. They felt that the extra work was warranted if there was any potential jeopardy to quality. Since they assumed that quality was driving the change, they had also not raised concerns about the extra work or reduced output to their supervisors.

None of the supervisors were aware of the specific problem that was reducing output. All they knew was that on a daily basis, they would first call the engineer's desk and get a recording that he was out of the plant working a new product issue. They would then send an electronic message to the owning engineer, assuming that he would read the message that day.

Upon further investigation, Mary later found out the engineer's laptop computer had somehow been infected with a virus that caused it to shut itself down. He had not attempted to contact the factory via phone or by using another PC for the entire time that he was out of the plant addressing the concerns over the new product.

4) Inconsistent Interpretation and Discipline

Background: Just as there had been inconsistencies identified in the treatment of the equipment maintenance technicians and the operators, there appeared to be an even bigger difference in the treatment of hourly employees outside the factory as compared to the treatment of those inside the factory. In the process of addressing another issue, Mary had been invited to attend an engineering management meeting on November 12. During the course of that meeting, a series of questions arose regarding the "unfair treatment" that one engineering manager felt had been given an engineering technician who worked for another engineering group.

Apparently, the engineering technician in question had voiced her concern about being required to have a meeting with her supervisor "just because she exceeded the personal absence hour allotment." She realized that the company's policies and guidelines dictated that she be disciplined. However, even though there had been no discipline, she found it to be insulting that her supervisor would even have the audacity to require her to meet with him over such a ridiculous policy.

A heated discussion followed. All of the engineering managers in the room took the position that the one remaining manager should have his supervisor apologize to the technician for creating an unproductive working environment. They had a multitude of reasons for taking this position, including the fact that the corporation was much bigger now and the policy was a leftover from the "days when ARI was a smaller company." Others felt that their managers and supervisors just didn't have the time to waste tracking attendance. Besides, the engineering departments were full of professionals. Engineering professionals were simply not like the factory employees.

The discussion took about half of the allotted meeting time. Mary was never asked to share her thoughts and ideas on the subject, nor did she volunteer to do so.

That portion of the session ended without resolution of the question at hand. Finally, the manager agreed to "work with Human Resources" to develop a kinder approach. He committed to adhere to that kinder approach once it was defined.

Issue #3—Meeting Commitments:
Follow-up and Follow-Through

Jim and Mary had many examples to support this category. In fact, they both felt that those examples included their own personal failures.

1) Closure on Communications

Background: Mary and Jim agreed to place themselves as the first example in this category. As a result of their actions, the factory employees were beginning to behave as if they no longer had as much trust in management. The employees were also beginning to complain to each other rather than raise issues to management. This was undermining the productivity within the factory work environment. Jim and Mary knew that changing this started with themselves and their actions.

Jim and Mary selected their personal failure as managers to respond to the pages and pages of issues and concerns that sat on the table before them. These were issues and concerns that had been raised by the employees within the factory. While they each knew that there was an unwritten requirement to provide closure to those issues, most remained open. Worse yet, in many cases there was no closure even when all that was required was for Mary or Jim to simply go back to the employee and communicate that nothing could currently be done about the concern that had been raised. Neither Mary nor Jim had made a habit of completing that closure step.

There were many, many examples.

In one case, the employee had come to Jim with an issue that was bothering him. Pre-assemblies entering his work area had a small trailing piece of plastic still attached to them. Apparently, the hydraulic cutter at one of the previous steps needed its blade aligned or replaced. Rather than assigning the closure to the employee, Jim had accepted the task himself. He was planning to visit that location during his next factory visit. Jim told the employee that he would take care of the problem that day.

Just as he was leaving that part of the factory, Jim was summoned to a last-minute product quality meeting. He changed his focus to understanding the customer concern at the quality meeting and forgot to write down the need to go back and close the issue, as he had committed.

A few days later, Jim received a sharply worded note from the operator who had originally complained. In his note, the operator mentioned that Jim was the last in a long series of managers who said a lot and committed to do a lot, but never followed through on their commitments.

The employee complained that "since Brian had bought out the 'old man'," things had been different. He did not like the changes and felt that if he couldn't believe what management said, he was doomed to failure. The note was six pages long and reflected a high level of frustration about everything from the temperature of the water coming out of the water cooler, to the ugly colors of the walls in the break room, to factory windows which were never cleaned, to his inability to get a competent equipment maintenance technician to perform repairs on his equipment. Everything was broken or falling apart. The work environment was intolerable.

Jim immediately scheduled time with the distraught employee. After about sixty minutes of hearing more of the same, the meeting ended. Jim apologized for failing to close the issue. He also agreed to complete the closure since the employee had done nothing further himself.

The knife was realigned that afternoon.

2) Closure of Assigned Action Items

Background: On October 10, Mary and Jim were reviewing the minutes from the last "all-hands" meeting that they had held with all of the factory's employees. Attendees had included operators, equipment maintenance technicians, and supervisors. In reviewing their notes, they noticed that several action items had been assigned and accepted by various attendees. While most of those that had been assigned to the equipment maintenance technicians were now completed, virtually all of those that had been assigned to the operators and supervisors remained open. In fact, among those action items that Mary and Jim were aware of, they could not recall seeing action of any type on any issue.

A quick call to two or three of the action item owners revealed that their assessment was correct. Indeed, no time had even been invested by a single action item owner. When asked why they were delinquent in completing the action items, or at least in informing those who would be affected by the lack of action, there was no response. None seemed to view the action items as critical. Further, none seemed to view keeping those stakeholders who would be affected informed of progress or delays as a needed action, not even from a courtesy point of view.

3) Assumed Individual Ownership

Background: During his last meeting with Jim, Darin had shared an incident regarding the compromising of product quality in the factory. Darin was obviously concerned about what had happened. On August 29, Darin had been in the factory. He happened to stop by a piece of equipment where an operator was quietly working away at her job. She seemed to be upset about something, but she wouldn't share any information about the problem. After spending a few minutes talking with her, Darin moved on to other things, forgetting about the discussion.

A few days later he received an e-mail message from the operator asking for a meeting in a private location. Darin offered to meet the operator in Conference Room A. Darin arrived at the designated time, but the operator was late in arriving. She indicated that she had waited until one of her coworkers returned late from lunch to relieve her.

After the usual pleasantries, the operator asked Darin whether anyone cared about the quality of the product that was coming out of the factory. Darin had assured her that everyone should be, and most were very concerned. He also assured her that he personally held quality above everything, with the exception of safety. She acknowledged that she believed Darin did care, and indicated that the reason she had selected him for this discussion was his commitment to quality.

The operator then relayed a series of recent incidents in which she had observed a small, closely-knit group of operators catching and fixing quality problems for each other. She was concerned that they were not following the designated process, which required the completion of a Quality Report by anyone who discovered a product quality issue of any kind. The Quality Report also ensured that appropriate quality tests and inspections were added to the process for that product whenever it was appropriate. In this case, they would simply let each other know that they had discovered a problem. The group would then come together and do a quick repair and send the product on as if nothing had happened. The product then continued through the factory until it was completed, packaged, and ultimately shipped to a customer.

The operator said that she simply wanted Darin to know and asked that her name remain anonymous. She did provide some names for Darin to begin his investigation if he chose to do so. The operator thanked him for his time, asked again that her name remain anonymous, and left the room without asking for anything specific to be done.

Darin had done some preliminary investigating by the time he brought the issue to Jim's attention. His information seemed to support most of the concerns that had been raised. He found that not all errors went without Quality Reports, but he also found that several engineers were concerned about the quality of work that was performed by that group of operators. One engineer was able to relate a specific incident that directly corresponded to the story that the operator had told him. When asked why he had not brought it to the attention of any of the production supervisors, the engineer indicated that he had taken care of the issue himself. He did not want anyone disciplined or fired over that single incident. To his knowledge, there had not been a repeat on his equipment.

Issue #4—Day-to-Day Operations

While it seemed so obvious, many of the biggest issues Jim and Mary identified had to do with the day-to-day operation of the factory. The majority were associated with things that Jim and Mary had just plain taken for granted as having been covered. To their surprise, that was not the case.

1) Equipment Downtime

Background: There were many examples of the equipment maintenance technicians being totally unaware that equipment was not operating properly or that equipment was down and needed their immediate attention. Mary had personally investigated several of the reported incidents. In each case, it appeared that the equipment maintenance technicians had followed the defined equipment status process by generating a request for an impromptu equipment status report. Investigation further revealed that the automated equipment-tracking feature in the shop floor control program took approximately fifteen minutes to run an impromptu equipment status report once a report request had been generated by the equipment technician.

The defined and documented process required that the equipment maintenance technicians use the impromptu report feature of the shop floor control system to assess all equipment status information. While it would have taken them only one or two minutes to walk around their specific assigned area within the factory and assess the status of the equipment, the defined process took fifteen minutes.

Rather than simply standing around and not doing anything during that report time, the technicians had adopted the pattern of sending in an equipment status query report request. They would then go on a coffee break. Unless something else happened, such as a request to help another technician handle a difficult equipment repair problem (which appeared to happen about 50% of the time), the report would be ready at almost exactly the same time that the technician returned from coffee break.

While Mary and Jim were unable to quantify the number of lost hours of output that this process was causing, they did know that it was significant.

2) Factory Cleanliness and Housekeeping
Background: On October 11, one of the technicians happened to see Jim in the break room taking a late lunch. She walked over and asked if he was aware that the pre-feed angle rod was shut down and that as a result, the front of the factory was totally shut down while waiting for work to be processed.

Jim asked some questions to gain a more thorough understanding of the situation, and then went looking for one of the production supervisors to get the details and to see if there was anything that Jim himself could do to help. No sooner had he stepped into the hallway than 'an excited Dawn had almost run him down.

"Slow down," Jim said, grabbing her before she ran into the now open door.

"Sorry. You'll never believe what happened!" Dawn said breathlessly. "The ...the ah, the rod ...Let me catch my breath." Dawn took a deep breath and then continued. "The pre-feed angle rod has been down all day. Apparently someone lost the master bolt while taking care of a problem that came up during the pre-flight. Anyway, we didn't have any master bolts left in the equipment back-up parts area, so everyone has been looking high and low for the one that was lost. Well, guess what?" Before Jim could say anything, Dawn went on. "They found the lost bolt in a pile of papers that were left over from yesterday. We lost six hours of factory processing time, and the bolt was sitting there right in front of them the entire time! I can't believe the luck."

"Have you replaced the bolt, completed the pre-flight, and started to run yet?" Jim asked.

Dawn nodded. "The first assembly should be coming off right now. But Jim, of all the stupidity! I'll be disciplining some people over this one, you can count on that!"

"Before you go disciplining anyone, maybe you can answer a few questions for me," Jim said. "What was the problem that caused them to need to tear down the equipment during the pre-flight?"

"Oh, it was a simple jam. The procedure calls for a complete tear-down as a precaution. I tried to get them to forget the pre-flight and just start running this morning, since we were so far behind. If they had listened to me, this would have never happened! A complete tear-down for a jam – it doesn't make sense to me."

"Dawn, there's a reason for pre-flights. Are you saying you would be willing to potentially jeopardize the quality of the product that we build today over the few extra minutes that it takes to perform an equipment pre-flight?"

"Of course not," an embarrassed Dawn replied. "I do understand the importance of the equipment pre-flights. I always try to make sure they're performed. It's just that we're so far behind."

Jim stroked his chin thoughtfully, trying to make sense of the situation. "What were the papers that were sitting on top of the bolt, anyway?"

"The paperwork was from yesterday's shift. There were logs and tracking sheets for the equipment, and some quality forms, I think. We were so far behind yesterday that the operators decided to work right up until it was time to go home last night. They didn't have time to turn in the logs and tracking sheets before they left.

"The operators planned on turning them in right after they completed the pre-flight and had the equipment up and running this morning. They're so far behind and so busy that they don't always have the time to pick up everything and put things away after they use them. The work area is so cluttered that they spent some extra time just getting their tools ready and getting the right paperwork located to start this morning. Then they ran into the pre-flight problem and couldn't find the area tear-down cart. Someone just decided to put the bolt on the table. Someone else slid yesterday's paperwork over on top of the bolt when they were trying to get to the phone. The bolt was buried somewhere under all of the clutter." Dawn shrugged and threw up her hands helplessly. "Anyway, one thing led to another, and this is where we ended up."

"It sounds like we have more than one problem to address here," said Jim. "Let's make sure that we get the right support for the operators. We can't afford to have the pre-feed angle rod down any longer. Is there someone else who can help with the paperwork? When are we going to start working to eliminate the clutter you mentioned?"

"Right away, boss."

Just then, Brian came up and started asking Jim questions about the rumor that the factory was not running again.

Jim asked Dawn to return to the factory and get someone to help sort out the previous day's paperwork and deliver it to the correct location as soon as possible. He also asked her to let him know how the area was running on an hourly basis for the rest of the day.

3) Daily Start-up Meetings

Background: Mary and Jim noted that many people had requested some kind of daily meeting to provide feedback and direction. Common reasons for this request included:

•   Daily priorities were unclear. Some days, different people seemed to be working to a variety of different priorities, causing confusion and inefficiency.

•   There was routinely a delay in communicating issues at the start of the day, which also led to confusion and extra work. Operators said they were often required to re-start or change what they were doing as a result of this delay. Many times this meant completely tearing down a set of tooling, installing the tooling for the new priority, pre-flighting the equipment, and then starting to operate. The operators frequently questioned whether management understood the huge amount of output lost as a result.

•   The delay in communicating problems was also affecting factory quality. Often the engineers or managers who were late in communicating the priorities and changes would ask the operators to hurry and make up time to cover for their mistake. This frequently included bypassing required checks and pre-flights. The operators said that they took these improper shortcuts because the direction was coming from a person of authority.

•   Many people were confused about what to do and when to do it. There was no easy way to see what the priorities were without examining the factory floor control master panel. This panel was available in three locations in the factory, but all three were far removed from most of the workers on the factory floor. Operators had the choice of waiting for a chance to walk to one of the panels, waiting for a supervisor to walk by, or talking to peers about what they thought the priority of the day might be. All of these led to inefficiency and time waste. Many led to wrong decisions. As was previously noted, operators and equipment maintenance technicians were confused regarding first their priorities, and next, the specific importance of the tasks that they performed.

4) On September 18, Jim had met with the team of operators and maintenance technicians who were responsible for the reverse wet flush area.

Background: Four frustrated operators arrived for the fifteen-minute sit-down meeting with Jim. The area equipment maintenance technician assigned to the area did not attend. He told his teammates that he didn't want to hear one more manager tell him what he already knew.

The meeting started with two of the operators blaming a third operator for causing all the problems they were experiencing in the their work area. That operator in turn blamed the equipment maintenance technician for the problems.

The fourth operator finally spoke up, after becoming noticeably frustrated hearing the team spend almost ten minutes complaining about each other. Her comments were simple, but drew nodding heads from everyone seated in the room.

"We don't know our priorities for the day until at least forty-five minutes after the shift has started. Almost half the time, we're asked to change what we're doing. We're told that we have the wrong priorities and that we are to immediately stop and switch over to the right priority.

"When all of us are there, it takes exactly thirty-six minutes to make a product switch. That's thirty-six minutes if everyone and everything is available and in the right location. If the right sub-parts haven't been pulled, that adds at least twenty minutes. If the product switch requires a complete tear-down and set-up, it takes exactly seventy-one minutes to perform. If we have problems, or if Julio, our equipment maintenance technician, is not available, it adds even more time. Add that seventy-one minutes to the forty-five minutes lost before we know about the change. We have about five or ten minutes until our first breaks start.

"Running with fewer people is a problem. Trying to recover lost output is almost impossible. As a result, we get told every day that we are the biggest problem in the factory."

5) Key Stations and Key Station Coverage

Background: The production supervisors had brought up a number of issues associated with providing appropriate coverage at key equipment and work areas. As business priorities changed, a change of priorities was often required inside the factory. This, in turn, often created staffing issues as operators and equipment maintenance technicians needed to be moved from lower priority assignments to higher priority assignments.

As a result of making assignments at the start of shift, then changing those assignments to accommodate the right priorities, operators and equipment maintenance technicians were routinely asked to change their break and lunch schedules after they had already made personal plans and arranged coverage. This caused major equipment coverage issues. It also created ill will within the workforce, as the employees' preference was to go on breaks and lunches with friends.

6) The Importance of the Work of Every Person and Team.

This was the one area that lacked examples with specific measurable impacts to performance. However, Jim and Mary agreed that it was too important not to include.

Background: Ten different employees had stopped either Mary or Jim to ask questions regarding exactly how the work they performed affected the success of the factory. In most cases, they assumed that the tasks they performed were not important to overall success, and this was almost always an incorrect assumption. Since decisions were being made on a daily basis regarding what tasks to perform, in what order to perform those tasks, and when to perform them, Mary and Jim agreed that these misperceptions were directly impacting the performance of the factory.

This same confusion affected the results achieved by various small teams working within specific areas of the factory. Often, members within the team were working to different priorities. This led to individual and team inefficiency. Many team members actually blamed each other for failing to meet the work area output goals. Some operators had become almost violent in their frustration when they were blamed for team shortfalls.

Issue #5—Employee Training and Development

1) Assignment and Training of Tasks

Background: On September 13, Mary was working in the factory with one of the equipment maintenance technicians when she happened to notice that the flying backlash machine had required equipment maintenance technician support three times during her fifteen-minute visit.

The flying backlash was one of the last process steps in the factory workflow. It followed a manual assembly step and fed its work to final assembly, which was followed by an inspection step and then prepackaging.

Upon investigating, Mary found that there was a timed reset button on the flying backlash machine that timed out every time a pre-assembly piece sat on the incoming feeder for more than 29 seconds. The actual flying backlash operation took 24 seconds. The manufacturer had included this timing function to ensure that output through the machine met specifications. The flying backlash machine operator was expected to be able to complete the operation on the current pre-assembly, and then push the release button on the incoming feeder to release the next pre-assembly for processing before the machine timed out. Experiments at the machine manufacturer's factory had demonstrated that the operator could perform the entire assigned machine processing tasks with about two or three seconds to spare.

The Amber Rose factory had two of the flying backlash machines, each with a dedicated operator. With four operators working the manual assembly step that fed the flying backlash machine, in theory there should have been an almost perfect match in timing. Thus, the workflow through both areas was maximized.

Only three operators were trained and on-site for the manual assembly operation during that particular shift. There were normally two other trained operators in the factory. During this shift, one was on vacation and the other was home with a severe cold. This created an uneven and often interrupted flow of pre-assemblies into the flying backlash incoming feeder.

Shutting down one flying backlash machine would have created a large queue of work waiting to be processed. The operators had been instructed to maximize output, since the work order that they were building was already three days past due and the customer was angry. Therefore, both remained at the flying backlash machines. Patricia had also requested that whenever there was nothing on the incoming feeder, the operator should move down the line and help at inspection, since they were finding several quality problems and were getting further behind as the hours passed.

The reset buttons were going off because the time required for a flying backlash operator to walk down the assembly line and conduct an inspection of one assembly, then walk back to the flying backlash machine, was averaging over 90 seconds. Periodically, that meant the remaining flying backlash machine operator would get behind.

Standard operating procedure required that when the reset button was tripped, only a qualified equipment maintenance technician could perform the reset function. This was a simple task with absolutely no risk, had the operator been allowed to perform the reset.

The good news: everyone was following the documented process. The bad news: the machine automatically reset based on the manufacturer's theory of through-put time.

Both the operators and the equipment maintenance technicians were clearly frustrated by the defined process. They were all proud of their strict adherence to documented process, however. When asked why this was not raised as a concern, the operators and equipment maintenance technicians told Mary that they felt they should never question a documented process.

When she asked how long it would take to train another back-up operator to cover for shifts when two were absent, Mary was told that it would take only about two shifts, as the operation was very simple. She was also told that it closely resembled the operation of the Mujinko thruster, and that the extra operators at that station could easily be trained to do everything in about two hours.

When she asked about transferring the reset function to an operator, Mary was told she should talk with Frederick, the equipment/process engineer. The equipment maintenance technicians and the equipment supervisors had previously tried to convince him to allow the change. The vendor had even suggested that it should be an operator task. Frederick had explained to all who asked that his equipment was too complex and important to have an operator doing resets.

The September 13 issue caused significant impact at not only the flying backlash area, but to the factory as a whole. Because the equipment maintenance technician was constantly being pulled from other repair work, other equipment that was needed to meet the day's output goal remained unavailable for use.

2) No Training Plans or Training Materials

Background: On October 9, Mary discovered that no one had been trained to operate the new mixer on the paste dispenser. Further, she found that no training materials were even available. The manufacturer of the paste dispenser had promised to provide a representative to conduct the training, but at the last minute the person had gotten sick. No one had reported this problem to either Jim or Mary. When Mary had asked the supervisors, they told her that with all the problems involved in just getting it to dispense paste, there hadn't been time to worry about training.

Mary contacted the paste dispenser manufacturer about the problem. While they could provide the training materials, there was no one who could provide training for at least two weeks. The manufacturer pointed out that while the model 2460 looked much different, the controls were in exactly the same spot as the model 1960, which this dispenser had replaced. They also promised to overnight express the training materials to Mary.

The ARI equipment engineer assured Mary that the controls were in exactly the same location. He felt that there was no need to worry about the delay in training and offered to make himself available if there were any training questions.

Jim sat back and surveyed all that they had accomplished that morning. Although the list seemed daunting, he felt confident that they could successfully tackle each primary issue by taking it one step at a time.

His confidence faded when he caught Mary's expression. Clearly, she was feeling overwhelmed. She sat motionless, staring at the table in front of her. Jim sensed that the magnitude of their work was hitting her all at once, and she looked as if she had run into a wall. All the energy she had displayed during their brainstorming session seemed to have drained out of her.

After a long silence, she met his gaze. "Jim, this is impossible. You and I both know Brian isn't going to give us enough time to fix all these problems. And we both know we can't get all of them fixed in just one or two weeks. I must have been crazy to agree to work on this. I should have left this morning. It's just like I told you it would be – all you've done is postpone the inevitable."

Jim put both hands on the table and leaned toward her. "Please slow down! We need to do more work to narrow this list down to a more manageable size."

"Manageable? Nothing's manageable when it involves Brian. How can we even imagine that he'll listen to us present this list without yelling? I can't believe I committed to helping you with this. What am I going to do?" She put her head in her hands.

"We can't solve every problem in the world at the same time," Jim said. "We need to determine which problems are the critical few that will make the greatest impact, and focus our efforts on those. We'll implement the actions that will have immediate positive impacts."

"But, Jim ...this is impossible," Mary reiterated, shaking her head.

"No, it's not. After we have the quick, high-impact actions in place, then we'll go after the long-term, permanent actions. This is not going to be completed in one or two weeks. It took months and years for all of these issues and problems to develop. It's only reasonable to expect that it will take weeks, and maybe months, to solve them. But Mary, we can have an immediate positive effect on things. We can take some actions immediately that will allow the factory to begin meeting some of its goals."

Jim took a deep breath and studied Mary's face. At least she seemed to be listening.

"In fact," he went on, "if we do this correctly, I think we can have a factory that's meeting output and quality goals within the next two or three weeks and performing at levels we've never seen before. Look how basic some of our problems are! Mary, we can do this. I'm more encouraged than ever after this meeting."

Jim paused long enough to give Mary time to process his words. He couldn't let her quit after all the work they had done; he would do everything in his power to prevent that from happening.

"I just can't face listening to Brian's reaction when he sees this list," she said at last. "I'm going to his office right now to tender my resignation." She began gathering up her things.

"Mary, I never thought of you as a quitter," Jim said, his heart pounding. "I can't believe you would give me your word and then back out on me. If you feel that there's no other option but to quit, then quit. But I think you're missing the significance of what we're doing for everyone at Amber Rose. Of all people, I thought you would consider the well-being of the employees as your number one priority. I'm disappointed in you."

Mary kept her eyes downcast.

"Staying or leaving is up to you," he went on. "It's your decision. But I do believe that Brian will support us in our proposal. Sure, he's going to ask hard questions and challenge us every step of the way, but we have the right answers. I believe we can make the factory a success. Brain won't turn away from a proposal that leads to success. He wants it more than any of us."

Jim watched Mary as she spent a quiet minute thinking about what he had said. Gradually he saw her expression change from one of fear and frustration to agreement.

"I guess you're right," she said finally. "We probably can do it if we stick together. There are a lot of problems, but many of them could be solved by getting back to the fundamentals of good factory operations and management." She paused and rubbed her eyes. "I think I'm ready to move on to the next step. But right now I'm really tired. It's been a long morning. How about a break?"

At 1:45 p.m., they adjourned the meeting and agreed to take a fifteen-minute break. At 2:00, they would bring in all of the supervisors. Together, they would proceed by identifying a still-to-be-named plan of action, which would include specific actions to address each category of problems.

Mary and Jim stood and stretched. They now had fifteen minutes to walk, relax, and shake off the cobwebs – a well-deserved break!

Chapter 6
The Plan Comes Together

The 2:00 p.m. meeting started precisely on time in Conference Room B. The supervisors were all present, as Jim and Mary had hoped. In contrast to the cramped conditions of CR-A, this room easily accommodated ten people, with room to spare. Three large windows overlooked the main parking lot. One entire wall held everything necessary to hold an efficient meeting: dry marker boards, flip charts, an overhead projector, and an assortment of pens, paper, and other accessories they would need to complete the work ahead.

As Jim entered the conference room, he couldn't help but notice that Mary and her supervisors, Devon and Jerry, had all taken seats on one side of the table, adjacent to the window. Darin and Patricia, who had once again arrived at a meeting ahead of Jim, had chosen seats on the opposite side of the conference table. Jim also noticed that all talking ceased as he entered the room and all heads turned in his direction. He sensed that they were waiting for his instructions and leadership, and hoped they were ready to tackle the tasks that lay ahead of them.

Jim and Mary had taken a few minutes to talk individually with each of the supervisors as part of their invitation to participate in the meeting. They all had been told that their participation and input would be critical in the development of the factory's recovery action plan.

Jim and Mary had requested that each supervisor think about the critical few changes that they felt would move the factory to new levels of performance. They asked each supervisor to come to the meeting fully prepared, ready to put all of their energy and creativity into developing an action plan that would turn the factory's performance around.

After seating himself next to Mary, Jim looked around at the attentive faces. "Within one week, the factory needs to be consistently meeting both output and quality goals," he said. "The purpose of this meeting is to develop a recovery action plan that will result in that outcome. I'd like to start by asking each of you to state how you feel you can add value to this action planning effort. Darin, would you like to start?"

Darin leaned back in his chair and shrugged. "Well, I think I can share my knowledge of what's gone on in the factory."

Jim nodded approvingly. "How about you, Patricia?"

She grinned. "I can rally the troops!"

Jim smiled at her enthusiasm. He went around the room to elicit responses from the others. Everyone gave their input, but Jim realized that some of them were sounding hesitant.

"Do all of you feel like you understand the desired outcomes of the action-planning meeting?"

No one responded. Jim waited, giving them time to think about it.

Finally, Patricia spoke up. "I think I can speak for the others. When I arrived for the meeting, I thought I understood. But now that you ask, I'm not really sure."

"I have some reservations," Devon added. "How can we develop an action plan in only a few hours? To complicate the task, it has to be an action plan that will fix a factory that has never really been properly performing to begin with."

Murmurs of agreement rose in the group.

"Let's discuss the purpose of the meeting for a minute," Jim said, trying to calm everyone down before feelings of gloom and doom settled in. He glanced at Mary for support. "We're here to continue the effort Mary and I started this morning. We've identified five categories of issues as a result of our personal observations of the factory's performance and based on the feedback we've received from our employees. That includes feedback from some of you. It will take the focused efforts of everyone in this room to develop an action plan that will meet the challenges the factory is facing. It will also take your full support and leadership to implement the plan. We need to give our total commitment to achieve the results we want. If you're unable to make such a commitment now or at any time during this meeting, you need to let Mary or myself know.

"The purpose of this meeting is *not* to rehash the past performance of the factory, but to set a course for the factory's future. That course will become our catalyst for future success."

The supervisors looked at each other and nodded. Patricia smiled at Jim supportively. Feeling somewhat reassured about the others' willingness to participate, he charged ahead.

"Okay, now that we're all on the same page," he said, "Mary and I will give you a brief summary of what has occurred so far."

Jim described his turning-point meeting with Brian and then encouraged Mary to summarize her own meeting with Brian and the subsequent meetings between herself and Jim.

As she spoke, Jim couldn't help asking himself if involving the supervisors was the right decision. They were all new to Amber Rose, and some were new to supervision. Was this the time to depend on people who didn't know the company, much less their jobs?

Jim's thoughts were interrupted by Jerry, one of Mary's equipment maintenance supervisors. "What do you plan on doing first?"

Jim handed out photocopied lists to the supervisors. "Mary and I have identified five main categories of issues." He glanced down at the paper in his hand as the others studied theirs. The five categories stood out clearly.

Issue #1—Communication

Issue #2—Policies, Procedures, Guidelines, and Expectations

Issue #3—Meeting Commitments: Follow-up and Follow-Through
Issue #4—Day-to-Day Operations
Issue #5—Employee Training and Development

Jim went on to explain how those categories would be used as the basis for the development of the factory performance recovery action plan. After he answered several questions, Mary continued where Jim had left off.

"Each category includes several significant issues to help clarify exactly what the category means," she said. "Jim and I are in agreement that the categories are the most important issues that we face as a factory. These issues must be addressed before the factory can operate effectively."

The other attendees nodded their heads in agreement. Encouraged, Jim and Mary continued with their plan.

Since Brian had been clear about his expectation of seeing immediate results, Mary had agreed to use Jim's two-pronged attack. The first phase focused on the highest priority categories and would include the immediate, short-term actions that could be taken to address those issues. The second phase focused on all five categories and included completion of the short-term actions, as well as the addition of a set of longer-term actions. In their meeting with Brian, they had planned to propose that all of the actions would be in place no later than sixty days after receiving Brian's approval.

After spending more than 30 minutes reviewing the categories and examples and answering the supervisors' questions, they were ready to start the working portion of the meeting. They left the categories in the same order in which they had been placed during their earlier meeting. Everyone agreed to work from the first category to the last category. They also agreed to place no more than three actions against each category.

After covering this background information and agreeing to the process that would be used, Jim asked everyone to stand up and count off by twos. They looked at each other quizzically before pushing back their chairs. Following the count-off, Jim asked those with even numbers to move to the window side of the table, and those with odd numbers to move to the wall side of the table.

"What are you trying to accomplish with this game of musical chairs?" asked Jerry. "Aren't we here to solve a serious factory performance problem? Do you really think we have the time for this?"

Jim smiled to acknowledge the concern, and then gestured around the table. "Look at the seating arrangement before we made this move. We had Mary and her supervisors on one side. On the other side of the table, we had the production supervisors seated together. We want this to be a collaborative effort. That means that we all have to be able to work together. I expect the collaboration to start here and now. That's why you're moving around the table. I also expect the collaboration to continue into the future as the way that we all perform our day-to-day business. So let's start working together right now." He looked around the room. "Does anyone have further concerns about doing that?"

Jerry was nodding. "That makes sense," he said, and proceeded to move around to the other side of the table and sat down next to Patricia. "Well, Patricia, I guess we're a team," he added, glancing at her with a smile. "Let's get started."

After everyone had taken their chairs, Jim continued the meeting by quickly reviewing the first category that he and Mary had identified during their previous meeting.

Issue #1—Communication.

Jim gave them time to review the examples that he and Mary had come up with.

"Does everyone understand the background information and our next steps?" he asked.

Everyone indicated that they felt grounded on the issues, and they all seemed ready to proceed. Patricia commented on how simple the actions were that they were developing.

They had gone through several of the issues and were concluding their work on the Day-To-Day Operations portion of the plan when Darin voiced a concern.

"These are too simple," he said, looking down at the notes spread out before him. "Most of the actions we've listed are really part of our everyday jobs – stuff that we should have been doing all along. Are you suggesting that the only issues we need to address are about getting back to basic operations – that all we really need to do is our job, and everything will be magically fixed?"

Jim rubbed his chin thoughtfully. "Darin, I think you've just named this program. We'll call it the ARI Winning Basics Initiative. You're right. Most of the issues we've listed should have been taking place all along. What we need to do is get Winning Basics, to perform the actions that are core to the success of any manufacturer. We need to make those a part of the way we conduct our business. Do you agree?"

Darin smiled proudly and nodded his head in agreement. With that, the meeting continued.

The results of two hours of work were remarkable. There were flip charts everywhere, and every marker board was covered with information.

The group's enthusiasm was somewhat dampened when Devon, who had been unusually quiet, spoke up.

"This is absolutely impossible," he said as he pushed back his chair and stood up. He strode to the front of the room and made a sweeping gesture with his arms, taking in the piles of documents scattered around the room. "Look at all this! You can't expect us to make all these changes. Some of the things you're changing have been the standard practice for years. People won't accept it. This plan is ridiculous!"

Jim opened his mouth to speak, but Jerry was ahead of him.

"You know, Devon, it'll be up to all of us to make this change happen." Jerry stood and moved to the front of the room to stand beside Devon. "It'll be up to all of us to make sure that everyone knows why we're making the changes. It'll also be up to us to make the changes happen with the smallest possible impact on our people. I've never been given the opportunity to be a part of the planning and execution of something as big as this. Personally, I'm excited to be a part of the management team that will make this change happen. We are the factory's management team."

"It's just too much," was all that Devon had to say in response. He returned to his chair, shaking his head. Keeping his eyes on the floor, he put his head in his hands as if in total disbelief.

"Devon might be right," said Darin. He took off his horn-rimmed glasses and set them on the pile of papers in front of him. "Maybe we should ask for more time. Should we do this in smaller, more manageable pieces?"

Jim stood up to command their attention. He had to nip these doubts in the bud if they were going to succeed. He had to pump up the confidence of these supervisors so they didn't feel overwhelmed. He had to let them know that the course they had set before them was fully within their capabilities.

"One of the best ways to make change," he began, "is to drive a stake into the ground and say that from this day forward, we're changing things. Jerry is right. It's up to all of us as the factory's management team to lead this change. There is nothing that our people cannot accomplish if we give them the training, the tools, the time, and the leadership. We need to be clear in our communication with all of our people. They can't feel that any of us are questioning these decisions and our new direction. They need to know what we're doing and why we're doing it, and what it means to each and every one of them. This effort will only be a success if each of you steps forward and becomes the leader that I know you're capable of being."

Jim's words seemed to have an effect, although he wasn't sure that the supervisors were completely convinced. They nodded and looked down at their notes, and he proceeded to lead them in the plan development.

His concerns were validated later when a heated discussion arose concerning the issue of discipline and consistency. During the discussion, Jim looked around the room at one point. To the person, the supervisors seemed uncomfortable with the topic and upset that Mary and Jim had brought it up in the first place. Jerry was looking out the window, as if hoping that by not looking at Jim, the subject would be changed. Darin was staring at his shoes and shifting from side to side. Patricia's face had turned beet red, and her jaw was clenched.

Clearly, none of the supervisors wanted to continue the discussion. Jim knew he would have to promote some supervisor team building once the plan was implemented.

"Jim, this seems like an exercise in futility," Patricia finally said. "How can we be expected to do our job and all of these extras as well? I don't think you're being realistic about what you're asking us to do."

Jim leaned back in his chair, running a hand through his hair. "How do the rest of you feel about this? Let's go around the table and get your feedback."

One by one, the supervisors were given the time to present their thoughts and feelings, and Jim thanked them. Most of the concerns were, he felt, obstacles that would be overcome once they began to see immediate changes in the factory's performance.

"It's not going to be easy," he said, "but it'll be worth it once we've implemented the changes. If any of you ever have any doubts or concerns along the way, I want you to feel free to come to either Mary or me with them. We're part of the factory's management team, too."

Before Jim had even finished the sentence, he was interrupted by Darin, who was shaking his head. "Come on, Jim. Number one, I've been here long enough to know that Brian is not going to buy into this plan. Just how stupid do you and Mary think I am? I've been here for five months now. The production manager who was here when I arrived had worked with all of us to develop a plan to help recover some of the factory's backlog." He jabbed a finger in Jim's direction. "Do you know what happened when he presented the plan to Brian? After Brian tore the plan to pieces, he fired the manager on the spot. He fired him right there in the meeting, in front of all the supervisors who were here at the time. That's what will happen to anyone who's connected to this plan. I've got a family to support, and I can guarantee you that I've been applying for jobs ever since that happened. As soon as I get an offer, I'm gone."

Jim took a deep breath. He knew Darin's concerns were valid; Brian had abused and humiliated nearly every supervisor on the workforce. "How do the rest of you feel?" he asked, fearing the answers that he was about to hear.

Devon was the next to respond. "To be honest, Jim, I'm with Darin. I don't like the way people are treated at Amber Rose. If I'd known what things would be like, I never would have left my last job. But the job market is tight, and I haven't got any options but to stay here. If I must put my name on this, I will, but I don't want to be fired with you and Mary. You know Brian is going to fire you for bringing this plan to him. Guaranteed."

Patricia was nodding. "Even though I appreciate your efforts, I won't have my name attached to this. I've seen how Brian manages this company, and I can't afford to be without a job. Maybe you don't realize what a bad position you're putting me in by involving me in the development of this plan."

Stifling a sigh, Jim nodded to acknowledge Patricia's concerns and turned to Jerry.

"I'll support you," Jerry responded. "I believe we can make a difference. What I can't be a part of is a company where the factory performs so poorly. I'm paid well for my services, and I want to see Amber Rose succeed. If I'm fired for trying to help make things better, so be it. I'll take the risk. This is the right thing to do."

Jim couldn't believe how many times during the meeting Jerry had stepped forward to defend Jim and the direction that he was trying to go. What a relief to know there was at least one person who was already committed to making a positive change.

Mary interrupted his thoughts. "Jim, I need to talk to you privately. How about allowing the supervisors to take a ten-minute break?"

By the looks of the room, everyone was certainly in need of a break.

"Is everyone agreeable to taking a ten-minute break?" Jim asked. There was a universal nodding of heads. After a few sighs of relief, the supervisors rose from their chairs and filed out of the room. Mary looked down at her hands for a moment as she fidgeted with a folder that was lying on the table.

"Jim, I told you that I would invest one day," she said finally. "I've spent almost the entire day with you, and it's been one of the most emotional and difficult days that I can ever remember. I've heard what the supervisors have to say, and frankly, I agree. Brian is not going to accept this plan. He's going to yell and scream, and after that, he's going to fire both of us. I just won't allow myself to be subjected to another of his tirades, and that's final. I'm going to go pack up my belongings and turn in my resignation."

Jim felt all of their hard work and planning slipping away from him. He was amazed once again by the detrimental impact Brian's attitude was having on everyone who worked at ARI. Even when he wasn't in the room, he was able to sabotage their confidence and ability to move forward.

"Mary, I can't guarantee that Brian will approve of our plan," he said. "Or that we'll be able to meet all of his expectations fast enough, even if he does approve the plan. I also can't predict what he'll say or do when we make the proposal to him. I'm hoping that he'll be reasonable. I think it's possible that dealing with so many problems has caused him to react the way he does to his employees. If we can show him that there's a light at the end of the tunnel, maybe he'll listen. But I can't say for sure. All I can guarantee to you is that we're doing the right thing.

"Even more important is the fact that we're doing it the right way. We've received input from people across the entire organization, with Brian being the one exception. We're building the plan with the involvement of the supervisors, and we've included other experts as they were required during the session today."

Mary closed her eyes and began rubbing her temples. "I don't know what to do. I'm tired and confused. What would you do if you were me?"

Jim grinned. "You know the answer to that question. Unfortunately, I am not you. This is a decision that you need to make on your own. But Mary, please make your decision, and please stick with that decision once it's made. It would really undermine this effort to have the supervisors and everyone else thinking that you were committed to staying and making the plan work, and then have you leave the company. It is your decision, though. What do you want to do?"

Mary heaved a sigh and said, "I think I just need to take a walk and think about things. I need some time to make this decision."

Jim nodded in agreement, and Mary collected her paperwork and left the room. For a minute Jim sat at the table alone, mulling over what had transpired in the past few hours.

"Where's Mary?" was the first question Jerry asked when he returned to the conference room. Other supervisors asked the same question as they arrived.

Jim told them honestly that she was taking a walk and that she might not be returning to the meeting. He reminded them all that Mary had worked late the night before and had been one of the first people to arrive that day.

"We all have a hard job ahead of us," Jim reminded the supervisors. "Let's get started." He asked them to go around the room and recap one or two key points they had learned from the first part of the session. He captured their inputs onto flipcharts for use later in the session.

Mary returned after about 30 minutes, looking much more relaxed. As she came up to speed on the direction that the meeting had taken during her absence, she became more and more engaged in the discussion. Another two hours passed before Jim felt that they had a solid plan in hand and were ready to move ahead by presenting it to Brian.

At the conclusion of the development, Jim again encouraged the supervisors to share their thoughts.

Darin, who had originally been the most vocal opponent of the plan, now smiled confidently. "I feel pretty good about it now.

We've come up with specific steps to take, so it doesn't seem so overwhelming."

"Me, too," said Patricia. "I think we have a good plan. If Brian rejects it, then he's a fool." They all looked at each other and laughed, releasing a little tension.

Jim was relieved that there was now universal agreement with the plan. Mary and the supervisors also pledged their commitment to lead the efforts required to make the plan a reality once Brian approved it.

Jim recognized that with all of the changes they were proposing, success depended as much on the factory workforce understanding and supporting the efforts as it did on Brian's approval.

"Would one or two of you be willing to help develop a communication package that I can present at employee meetings?" Jim asked. Those meetings would include first the attendance of every factory employee, and then every ARI employee.

As had occurred throughout the meeting, Jerry was the first to volunteer, and Darin quickly joined him. Jim challenged their ability to commit, given all the action items that they had already accepted, but they didn't hesitate to remind him of the importance of making this effort a success. Mary asked to be a co-presenter at the sessions, but deferred to Jim regarding the actual development of the presentation package.

Before the supervisors left the room, Jim and Mary offered their sincere thanks for a job well done.

"You were all one-hundred percent engaged during this entire meeting," said Jim, "even when you disagreed or disliked the direction we were heading. I appreciate all your great insights and suggestions." Jerry, in particular, had done a good job of breaking up the many difficult topics with his lively sense of humor. Jim made a mental note to thank him privately for his support.

The supervisors shared their thanks, as well.

"I really feel that I've participated in something that's critical to the business here," said Patricia. "It was nice to have someone ask my opinion for a change."

The others agreed. They felt that there had been a genuine desire to seek and use their input, and they were able to see their ideas become a part of the proposed Winning Basics Initiative. All in all, though there had been some difficulties, they considered the meeting a success.

As the supervisors filed out of the conference room, Jim added, "Remember, this was the easy part of the job. Tomorrow we'll really need to get to work."

They had all committed to work into the evening to help complete the steps necessary to implement the agreed-upon action plan the next morning. They also knew that they were expected to be part of the team that first communicated the action plan to the factory workforce and then made it a success. That was assuming that Brian approved the action plan, of course.

Jim and Mary stayed behind after the supervisors had left. Taking a swallow of his lukewarm coffee, Jim realized that he had not yet eaten a full meal that day.

"Jim, mixing up the seating arrangement was a great idea," Mary commented. "We really got some excellent synergy. I wish I had thought of that before I sat down next to my supervisors. And I do appreciate you giving me the time to take a walk. I was at my wit's end. I needed to get away from this for a few minutes."

Jim smiled. "I understand."

"We've all known that the factory wasn't meeting expectations," she continued, "but we weren't able to really get our hands around the problems. Without having the problems clearly defined, there was no way to get the initiatives in place to address those problems. With all the new people, and all the extra tasks that we've been assigned at the morning production meetings, it's a wonder things aren't even worse."

Jim nodded in agreement. Privately, he still couldn't believe how basic the factory issues really were. *How could I have allowed this to happen?* he wondered.

"Well, enough reminiscing about the past," he said. "Let's get our notes ready and make the copies we'll need for our meeting with

Brian. How do you want to conduct the meeting? Do you want one of us to make the entire presentation, or do you want to share it?"

Mary shrugged. "We're in this together, aren't we?"

"Of course," Jim replied, knowing that a further response was not required from Mary. They were in this together. Jim just hoped that Mary was indeed committed. He was bothered by the number of times she had decided to quit so far.

"Then we share the presentation," was Mary's quick reply. "Now, let's get started preparing the materials."

They spent no more than 30 minutes summarizing the key categories and actions. They had worked through a rough process with the supervisors to quantify the amount of impact each action would have. Jerry had been very helpful, since he had a productivity calculation software program loaded on his laptop computer. Though the different variables were not always available, there seemed to be a general consensus during the meeting that the factory output improvement quantities assigned to each action were reasonable and achievable.

Jim took responsibility for consolidating everything into a single package. He planned to make three copies for the upcoming meeting with Brian.

After collecting the flipcharts and paperwork, he and Mary left the room, and Jim went straight to his desk to drop off his laptop and the paperwork. From there, he made a beeline for the factory. After spending about 30 minutes walking through the work areas, he took a minute to chat with each supervisor.

Back in his office, Jim condensed the summary they had developed into a one-page outline of the Winning Basics plan that they would present to Brian.

Amber Rose Industries
Winning Basics

A) COMMUNICATION
1.   All-Hands, Start-of-Shift Meetings
a)   Start of Every Shift
b)   Mandatory Attendance
c)   Production and Equipment Supervisor Share Leadership
d)   Set Agenda

2.   Communication Reader Boards
a)   Primary Location at Front of Factory
b)   Satellite Locations within Major Work Areas
c)   Hourly Updates

3.   Real-time Performance Tracking and Feedback
a)   At-Station Tracking Sheets
b)   Hourly Updates on Information

B) POLICIES, PROCEDURES, GUIDELINES &
     EXPECTATIONS
1. Development, Documentation, and Communications
2. Self-Discipline and Assumed Individual Ownership

C) MEETING COMMITMENTS
1. Closure on Communications
2. Closure on Assigned Actions

D) DAY-TO-DAY OPERATIONS
1. Quality Control
2. Management of Priority Changes
3. Break and Lunch Station Coverage Planning
4. Communication of Products and Priorities
5. Rules that We Work By

6. Methods that We Follow
7. Equipment Downtime Tracking
8. Factory Cleanliness and Housekeeping

E) EMPLOYEE TRAINING and DEVELOPMENT
1. Factory Training Plan
2. Training Materials
3. Employee Training and Development Plans

Chapter 7

Taking the Plan to Brian

Jim met Mary outside Brian's conference room and gave her an encouraging smile.

"We can do this," he said as they walked in.

Brian stood at the window, looking outside. It took Jim a moment to realize that Brian was watching a bird as it attempted to catch one of the koi from the pool below. Each time the bird dove toward the water, the fish disappeared under a rock, and the bird pulled out of the dive at the last minute. Then the fish moved out from under the rock, and the sequence was repeated. Brian was chuckling at the sight.

Jim and Mary waited until Brian noticed their presence. As he turned, he immediately became deathly serious. Jim and Mary sat down as Brian took his accustomed place at the head of the table. There they were, three people sitting in a room designed to comfortably seat twenty.

Jim and Mary had agreed before the meeting that no matter what Brian said, they would leave the meeting proud of the work they had done. They were proud of the team effort that their supervisors had put into the development of the proposal. Given the time constraints that had been imposed on them, they both felt that the team had done an excellent job of developing a sound factory recovery action plan – one that would truly make a difference in the performance of the factory. It was an action plan that they were both proud to present.

Since the preparation had taken most of the available time, Jim and Mary had decided to avoid the podium and audio-visual equipment, feeling that "Winning Basics" also meant not worrying about colored foils and fancy presentations. What was important was the content of the message they delivered.

Jim handed Brian a copy of the plan outline. He had attached the meeting materials from both the morning and afternoon meetings as back-up information should Brian have any specific questions about the process they had used, the criteria for selection of the categories, the data, or the expected improvements.

Jim took a deep breath and began. "Brian, we appreciate you taking the time to meet with us in private. We've been working all day with our teams to develop the proposal you're about to see. We've named our plan the ARI Winning Basics Initiative. Our team is unanimous in our agreement that we can start implementing these changes immediately. In fact, most of the changes can be implemented tomorrow. Further, we expect to begin seeing some positive results within twenty-four hours after implementation. It may take us a week or so to meet all of the production goals, but we're convinced that we can have this factory performing at higher levels than you have ever seen. You will see improvement within two weeks. We are also willing to commit to meeting or exceeding all of our monthly production goals for this month, even with the loss of one week." Jim paused and looked at Mary, who would begin with the prepared materials.

"As Jim said, we're calling our plan Winning Basics," she said, her voice trembling slightly. "This plan is focused on the basic, critical elements of manufacturing. Based on our information, we don't feel that there's a need to spend a lot of money on new tooling or equipment and supplies. Rather, we feel that we're not maximizing the effectiveness of the factory's resources, our people, and the equipment that we have in place. The reason for the Winning Basics name will become even more obvious to you as we continue to make this presentation."

Jim and Mary alternately presented the various topics. The conclusion, which was a review of all of the key points, they would present together.

Brian stopped them in the middle of their first topic – communication. Jim was concluding his description of the start-of-shift meetings when Brian held up a finger and said, "Excuse me, Jim."

Jim felt his defenses go up. Despite his earlier display of confidence with the supervisors, privately he was still worried that Brian would halt the meeting to attack their ideas without giving them a chance to make their case.

"These start-of-shift meetings will occur in the morning?" Brian asked.

Jim and Mary both nodded.

"Can you tell me how they will affect the morning production meetings with the supervisors?"

Jim relaxed as he realized that Brian was not criticizing but simply asking for clarification. As Jim explained, Brian listened and then let them continue once he understood. He stopped them several more times during the presentation, mainly to ask questions regarding the expected results and the timing associated with achieving those results.

Although he slipped back into his old ways a couple of times, Brian avoided questioning their competence or the competence of their teams. He didn't question the process they had used, or their choice of names for the categories, or the specific actions they had defined. In fact, he seemed to have come to the meeting with the goal of truly understanding the information they were presenting.

Jim took turns with Mary answering the best they could, relieved that Brian was making an effort to understand their points and the basis for their recommendations. He even thanked them for their responses, something Jim couldn't recall previously experiencing during his tenure at Amber Rose.

After Jim and Mary covered all of the prepared information, which took about 30 minutes, Jim felt even more strongly that they were offering a logical plan that directly addressed many of the problems Brian had been hearing about. Jim knew that employees across the organization had raised these issues to Brian many times. He and Mary made sure to indicate that the entire factory management team was behind this action plan. They had helped to develop the plan and were committed to achieving the results.

Once they were finished, Brian stood up and folded his arms, looking thoughtful.

"I like your proposal," he said after a pause. "It makes sense, and it's simple. I do appreciate all your work today. But you need to show me results this week, as you've committed. I need to have the factory performing to goal for the month." His eyes narrowed as they moved from Jim to Mary and back to Jim. "After that, there had better be no slips in performance. Do I make myself clear?"

Jim and Mary nodded.

"We fully intend to do just that," Jim said.

"Well then, it's your baby. Run with it." Brian slapped his hand on the tabletop to emphasize his words and then strode out of the room, closing the door behind him.

As Jim watched Brian leave, he felt a mix of relief and uncertainty. Although the session had gone well – even better than expected – he couldn't help but wonder if Brian was really willing to bet the business on the results they had committed to achieving.

"Well, that was certainly some meeting!" said Mary, the relief visible on her face. "What did you think? Did it go as well as you hoped?"

Jim nodded. "Pretty well. But we have a lot of work to do." That was all Jim could bring himself to say. It had been a long, hard day, and there were several hours of work ahead before Mary, Jim, or any of their supervisors would be leaving for the night. But he was gratified that their plan had been accepted and that they could now move forward.

"Are you ready to go to work?" he asked.

Mary nodded.

"Okay, then. Let's get the supervisors in here and start assigning owners and due dates to the action plan."

Mary nodded, then picked up the phone to start the process.

Back in his office, Brian settled into his plush executive chair and began to ponder his options. Though nobody else was aware of the situation, the bank was pressuring him to bring his late payments up to date, and there would be no more extensions. Other creditors were also beginning to threaten him with collection actions. The company was no longer able to cover its expenses.

Brian absolutely could not afford to lose another customer. He had to make some money. Otherwise he would have to shut the business down. The factory was the key to making the money he so desperately needed. There were still weeks' worth of orders that had been delayed due to factory performance. Delivering on those past-due orders would significantly change the financial situation he was facing.

Jim and Mary were offering a set of actions that they felt would show immediate returns. The answer seemed pretty straightforward when Brian thought about it. He couldn't afford to let either Mary or Jim leave, much less both of them. He knew that his methods had not been successful and that he needed to rely on the factory's expertise —and that meant Jim and Mary.

If only I had some background in manufacturing! he thought. *If only I hadn't bought this business last spring.*

He rubbed his face with both hands, willing the problems away. He knew he had no real choice but to follow Jim and Mary's lead.

Chapter 8
Winning Basics: From Plan to Action

As the supervisors began to arrive at the conference room, it was clear that the question on everyone's mind was, *Did you get Brian's approval?*

Jim and Mary could hardly hold back their excitement about getting approval to move forward. Neither had really expected that Brian would give his approval to the proposal as it was written. They had expected him to ask for many changes, or even turn down their request entirely. There had also been the strong possibility that the supervisors were right, and that Brian would fire them on the spot. To everyone's relief, that hadn't happened.

The last of the supervisors arrived within ten minutes of the first phone call Mary had made. She and Jim reported the results of their meeting with Brian and reviewed the five priorities and actions from earlier in the day. They planned to examine each action, one by one, until each had been thoroughly covered. As an action was reviewed, they would assign owners and due dates for implementation. This process also allowed the others to speak if they had additional questions or concerns after having had the afternoon to think about it.

Communication

First and foremost came communication.

Communicate, communicate, communicate—and then communicate some more!

Jim had heard those words so many times before, but here they were, with communication at the top of the list of issues that needed to be addressed. As they looked at the many consequences of poor communication among the workforce, whether too little communication or no communication at all, Jim couldn't help but silently chastise himself for failing to address this issue sooner. Brian or no Brian, Jim had known better than to let this happen. He'd known how to take care of this problem, yet he had just not done an acceptable job. Now there was a plan, and it was a plan that the supervisors had developed.

Action #1—All-hands, Start-of-Shift, Stand-up Communication Meetings

A short, stand-up meeting would be initiated at the start of every shift to address the requests for factory communication meetings, to ensure that everyone had the right priorities, and to ensure that all problems and issues were discussed. These meetings would be held in the factory and would require the attendance of 100% of the operators, equipment maintenance technicians, production supervisors, and equipment supervisors.

Every shift would start with one of these all-hands, stand-up meetings on the factory floor. Every attendee was expected to be at the meeting on time. The production and equipment maintenance supervisors would share leadership of the meeting equally. The meeting was expected to last no more than five minutes, so the supervisors were expected to arrive prepared and the meeting was expected to begin promptly at the start of each work period.

The supervisors agreed to an agenda for the first meeting. As they held meetings during the first two weeks, they would solicit feedback from the operators and equipment maintenance technicians about what was of most value to them. The supervisors would then meet for five minutes immediately following the all-hands, start-of-shift meeting. During that time, they would make the appropriate adjustments using attendee inputs, as well as their own. The first meeting's agenda included:

• Our last shift results—This included safety updates and information if required, quality updates and issues if required, total factory output, output through key equipment and work stations, and other key information from the previous shift that this team had worked. If the shift had achieved its production goals, this was designated as the time to recognize that achievement.

• Off-going shift last results—Amber Rose Industries had two shifts. Both worked a modified day shift. This agenda item would include most of the same information of the previous shift's performance. This item would be used to strengthen each shift's focus on the right tasks ahead. It would also build shift-to-shift interaction, as well as healthy inter-shift competition.

• Highlights of what is happening—This would identify the priorities and expected issues for the shift that they were just starting. Included in this would be information regarding equipment maintenance and unscheduled downtime, product priorities and potential quality issues, key equipment and work station status, staffing strategy, and other critical information that the supervisors felt must be communicated.

• Issues and Challenges expected at the start of shift—This was to include no more than two to four items and could include any information that the supervisors felt required everyone's focus.

- Other potential issues that might occur—This included such information as known upcoming changes in orders that were currently being processed. Until the factory was caught up, everyone expected multiple product changes to remain the way they performed their business. After all, meeting customer needs with good quality products in a timely fashion was the factory's responsibility.

- Ensure that all assignments are known—This included information about which operators would be working where, break and lunch coverage plans, and information about training assignments. The same information was communicated to the equipment maintenance technicians.

- Ensure that the current shift priorities are known—This was the last thing they wanted everyone to hear. This included the top three to four products and/or equipment and workstations that everyone needed to support through the upcoming work shift.

As Jim rose to place aside the flip charts that contained the agreed-upon information, Patricia said, "I've been thinking about this meeting. With that many agenda items, I think it'll take at least thirty minutes to hold the all-hands, stand-up, start-of-shift meeting. It just can't be done in the five minutes that we have targeted. I can't commit to communicating this much information that quickly."

Further discussion ensued, and they agreed to extend the meeting to ten minutes. Jerry raised his hand.

"I suggest we commit to preparing for the meeting in advance by having the information assembled and ready to communicate prior to the start of the meeting. We could even learn to be more concise by timing each other to make sure the meeting stays on track. What to do you think?"

The other supervisors all nodded their heads in agreement.

"Sounds like a good idea," Patricia said with a smile at Jerry.

Finally, they agreed to modify the agenda. They would discuss shift priorities and then break into appropriate smaller groups to communicate the staffing plans for that shift after the meeting was completed.

Action #2—Communication
Reader Boards

Three-by-five-foot reader boards were to be installed in visible places throughout the factory. Daily targets for the equipment and work areas within that portion of the factory were posted at the top of the reader boards. Hourly updates, noting whether the factory was on schedule, ahead of schedule, or behind schedule were then added. This updating task assignment was to be rotated through all members of the factory team.

The primary factory communication reader board would be installed at the front of the factory. That board would contain the following information:

• **Shift Priorities**—This was to be a written version of the shift priorities that were communicated verbally during the start-of-shift stand-up meeting. This information was to be posted by the supervisors.

• **Safety**— If there were any safety updates or issues, they were to be posted on the communication reader board.

• **Quality**— Quality issues were to be posted as soon as they were known. Any changes that might jeopardize quality were also to be posted in advance of those changes being implemented.

• **Output**—Every two hours, the total output completed so far during that shift for key equipment and workstations would be posted. Total factory output completed so far during the shift would also be posted. Initially, the supervisors would post this information, with the goal of transferring maintenance of the factory updates to one or two operators in the future.

•   **Changes**—Any time a change in priorities occurred, it was to be immediately posted on the communication board by the supervisors. They all agreed that placing new information on the communication board did not replace the need to verbally communicate all key changes to the right factory personnel. Adding the information to the communication board was merely an additional means of communicating critical information to all who needed to know that information.

•   One corner of the communication board was to be left as a message center. This space was available if someone had a general question about a product being built, or had an issue that was not urgent but required communication with a supervisor, or if there was some general information that the supervisors wished to communicate.

Placing communication reader boards throughout the factory seemed like an easy thing to do. It also addressed the need for ongoing communication and updates. There was very little discussion after the information list was reviewed. Jerry volunteered to secure the communications reader boards, and to have them installed within twenty-four hours after receiving them.

Action #3—Real-time Performance Tracking and Feedback

Everyone agreed that there was presently no easy way for the factory's personnel to obtain much-needed real-time information about individual equipment or work area performance. While the communication reader boards would help to provide additional information, something more was needed. After a short discussion that included a brief examination of the current systems that might support this action, it was agreed that a short-term and then a long-term response would be required.

For the short-term, at-station tracking sheets would be implemented throughout the factory. These sheets were to be placed at every piece of equipment and in every work area to give the operators a way to easily keep track of their output throughout the work shift. The sheets would include daily goals with hourly updates. If the operators were behind on their schedule, there had to be a plan for catching up. The supervisors agreed to periodically go to the various work areas throughout the work period and either provide positive feedback if the operator was on-track for output, or provide coaching and support if the operator was behind on scheduled output.

"Is anyone willing to volunteer to create the tracking sheets?" Jim asked. "I'd like to have them in use on the factory floor for the next scheduled shift."

Darin raised his pen in the air. "I can do it. I could also develop a brief overview regarding why the change is being made, and an introduction to the tracking sheets and how to complete them."

"Thank you, Darin. Can each of you then present the overview information to each work area team during that first shift?"

The supervisors nodded.

"And Darin, if you will, I'd like you to provide every supervisor with copies of the tracking sheets and the other information, as well."

"No problem."

As a long-term action, the supervisors agreed to provide easily accessible, real-time output information in every work area of the factory.

"This approach will require support from the Information Systems group, as well as money approval from Brian," Jim explained. "Programming changes and additional computer terminals will also be required to successfully implement the long-term changes."

Just as the equipment maintenance technicians ran into long time delays when using the impromptu report feature of the shop floor control system to assess equipment status, so did those requesting output or quality data. Exactly the same delay occurred when operators requested output data for their equipment.

There were additional issues, as well. First, there was a limited number of locations where impromptu reports could be requested. Also, the system was only capable of handling the processing of five requests at a given time.

"Does everyone agree with the short-term action we've settled on?"

The supervisors each gave their approval.

"It's quick, easy, and doesn't require much spending," said Darin.

"How about the long-term actions?"

Mary spoke up. "I'll assume responsibility for the long-term actions."

Jim nodded appreciatively. "Thank you, Mary. Please feel free to call on the supervisors and myself for support as needed."

Policies, Procedures, Guidelines & Expectations

The way Jim saw it, this portion of the plan meant establishing a shared understanding of the company's policies, procedures, guidelines, and expectations. He intended to focus first and foremost on management consistency and adherence. The greatest responsibility clearly fell on the supervisors. Ultimately, they were responsible as a first-line management team to maintain consistency in both their interpretation and enforcement of these items.

Of all the categories contained in the action plan, Jim knew that those requiring self-discipline and shared ownership would be the most difficult to address. The supervisors needed to be consistent in their interpretation, in their communication, and in their practices.

First, however, Mary and Jim were responsible for facilitating this shared understanding which the supervisors needed to achieve.

This topic met with much discussion and much disagreement. After having had some time to think about the solution that had been identified in the earlier meeting, some of the supervisors had become very defensive. They felt that they were already the correct interpreters of the policies, procedures, guidelines, and expectations. Their solution was simple: all others should just change their interpretations and practices to match.

"I've been here the longest, and I just don't see why I'm the one who needs to change," said Patricia. "Why can't Darin relax and treat his people as though he cares about them?" Darin opened his mouth to defend himself, but Patricia went on. "What's the big deal, anyway? We all know that the equipment maintenance technicians are allowed to arrive late. They're also allowed to leave early. And how many of us don't know of an equipment maintenance technician who's taken an extra long break – and an extra break, for that matter? What's fair for the equipment maintenance technician is fair for my operators. I don't care what you say, Darin."

"Okay, Patricia," Jim interjected, putting his hands up. "I hear what you're saying. But our people are telling us that we're inconsistent, and I've noticed it, too. What do the rest of you think?"

After about five minutes of disagreement and discussion, Jim suggested that they take a new approach.

"How about if we assume that none of us really knows the policies, procedures, guidelines, and expectations at Amber Rose? We could all be trained in them together. Then we could come to some basic agreements as to how we'll handle the more common situations. What do you think?"

After a few seconds, heads started to nod in agreement. The more the supervisors thought about this idea, the more enthusiastic they became.

"We can address the way tardiness is mistreated," Darin suggested, looking directly at Patricia.

"That's right," Patricia responded, returning his direct stare.

"Okay, okay, I get the message," Darin said with a little smile. "I'm sorry, Patricia. Let's see what we learn by reviewing the materials. Then we can come to an agreement about exactly how enforcement of the policies and guidelines would best be addressed."

The rest of the supervisors agreed with that approach. They immediately agreed to the first action they would take to address the issues in this category.

Action #1—Develop, Document, and Communicate

Jim took ownership for scheduling two management-training meetings for all supervisors and managers within Amber Rose Industries. Attendance would be mandatory.

During the first session, Jim and Mary would thoroughly review policies and guidelines and answer all questions. Then every supervisor and manager would have a chance to apply the reviewed materials by working through a set of life-like scenarios on the various policy and guideline topics. Jim knew that he could work with Jane Donaldson, the human resources generalist, to develop those scenarios.

The second management training session would be a working session with a focus on employee expectations. Jim and Mary would review established expectations. Then small teams of supervisors and managers would identify and document recommended changes to those existing expectations. Other small teams of managers and supervisors would begin assembling expectations where none currently existed. Together, the attendees would discuss, and then ratify, all changes, additions, and deletions.

Following the session and attendee ratification, Human Resources would conduct a comprehensive review of the recommended expectations. Approval from HR was again required before the recommendations went to Brian. Brian would complete the final review and give final approval.

Once the plan received Brian's approval, Jim and Mary would hold a follow-up session with all of the supervisors and managers. That meeting would be the last chance for every manager and supervisor to review the new expectations before they were communicated to the general employee population. During the review session, Jim and Mary would thoroughly explain each of the expectations. There would also be time during the meeting for an open forum, during which all questions would be answered.

Following the final management meeting and the open forum, Jim suggested general communication meetings with all of the company's employees. Those meetings would serve as an opportunity to communicate the new expectations. He and Mary would provide a comprehensive review of all expectations, as well as a review of the consequences for failure to adhere to those expectations.

Time would also be provided for all of the employees to ask questions and raise their concerns. Jim and Mary would allow time for every concern to be examined. Should a valid issue be identified, changes would be made to the expectations, and they would communicate those changes at a follow-up session. If no changes were warranted, Mary would send a personal message to each employee who raised an issue or concern, informing him or her of the final decision and explaining the basis for it.

Following the general communication meetings with the entire employee population, every supervisor and manager would meet with his or her direct reports. These final meetings would serve to ensure that no new questions had arisen. If there were new questions, the supervisors and managers were expected to provide answers during those final employee meetings.

From that point forward, all of management would be held accountable for consistently interpreting and adhering to the expectations, as they had agreed to do. Managers and supervisors would be directed to funnel all new questions to either their department managers or to the Human Resources department.

Action #2 —Self-Discipline and Assumed Individual Ownership.

Jim prompted discussion of this item by asking, "Does anyone know what self-discipline and assumed individual ownership means?"

The others remained quiet, looking at him expectantly. Darin finally spoke up.

"I think I know, but it's hard to put into words."

"That's okay," said Jim. "This category might be a little more intangible than the others. It has to do with creating an environment and culture that nurtures every employee in the direction of assuming more responsibility for the results the factory achieves. Many of the actions within the plan will start the factory down this path. If I didn't call out this category as a stand-alone item, nothing would ever happen. Developing consistency within the factory's management is a strong step in moving everyone forward along this path."

After much discussion, the supervisors finally agreed that this action was really more about making a statement about the environment that they all wanted to create in the factory. It was a vision for the future that included:

1) Open Communication

This meant more than just holding communication meetings; it included opportunities for two-way communication. This meant that any employee could share his or her ideas and concerns with every other employee. This also included sharing those ideas and concerns with Brian. Likewise, there were opportunities for Brian and his managers to communicate with all of their peers and with every employee throughout the organization.

This kind of environment should produce no surprises. Appropriate top priorities, company status, and other important information would be freely shared throughout the workplace. All employees would understand how their contributions supported the top priorities of the company.

2) Trust

It was easy enough to say the word trust, but establishing an environment that nurtured trust was an entirely different matter. While Jim recognized that this was a major gap in the culture at

Amber Rose Industries, he decided to put off efforts to correct that gap for now.

"We all own this," he told the supervisors. "It's our job to foster an environment in which our employees can raise issues and know that those issues will be taken seriously, without repercussions.

"It's also our job to foster an environment in which there is never retribution for making mistakes or suggesting solutions that do not work. Rather, we all learn from our mistakes and do our problem-solving in such a manner as to minimize the risk.

"Our proposed solutions in this plan should work. We all need to make sure the risk-taking that happens is always intelligent and informed."

Jim's last point on this topic focused on taking the first steps with the Winning Basics effort.

"We have many of the fundamental points identified throughout the Winning Basics plan. We all need to make sure that we begin to change the environment by demonstrating that we trust others and that we ourselves are trustworthy. We need to earn the trust and respect of everyone else at ARI. It all begins with us."

Those were the goals in terms of their shared vision for the future. They all agreed to put first priorities first, however. Therefore, they deferred specific actions associated with the creation of their future environment and focused all of their energies on the specific actions they had identified.

Meeting Commitments: Follow-Up and Follow-Through

The supervisor plan for this topic centered on creating an environment in which every employee felt the freedom to accept ownership for making things better at ARI. If an opportunity appeared to make an improvement, any employee who was capable, competent, and had the time to address the issue could step forward and begin that effort. It would be an environment in which employees sought out the problems, unlike the current environment in which people didn't accept ownership because they were afraid of the consequences. Everyone feared being blamed for the problem. In the future, if there were roadblocks hindering the factory's success, Jim hoped employees would seize the opportunity to remove those roadblocks.

Jim's personal vision was of a factory in which every employee was willing to commit to owning problems and issues as they were identified. It would be a factory in which every employee felt a sense of ownership and responsibility for making things better. Employees would willingly step forward to partner with management in removing the roadblocks that were hindering factory performance.

When the employees stepped forward to partner, or even to accept full ownership for problems and issues, there would be an infrastructure to support their problem-solving efforts. Employees would receive training in sound problem-solving techniques and processes and would have access to problem-solving coaches and mentors.

From a management perspective, developing absolute employee trust was the goal. Jim recognized that one of the strongest and most important actions that could be taken was to make and meet commitments. Management needed to demonstrate that when they made a commitment, they followed through. There would be clear communication of the exact nature of the deliverable and updates on progress made to date. Should there be changes in the committed deliverable or the committed delivery date, those changes would be communicated as soon as they were identified. Management would always drive to true and complete closure on their commitments. Finally, when there was not going to be delivery on a request, management would step forward and communicate to the appropriate people – and management would explain why.

Making and meeting commitments was one of the strongest ways that managers could demonstrate their trustworthiness. This was another obvious issue. Mary and Jim both knew that they themselves were guilty of not being good role models of this behavior.

Action #1—Closure on Communications

Jim and Mary understood that just as this issue started with them and their past practices, the action associated with this issue would also have to start with them. They owned going back and closing with every employee on every issue they had reported. To accomplish this, Jim and Mary would review their notes for the last 60 days and note every idea or concern that an employee had raised. If they knew the name of the person, they would make immediate closure with that person.

They developed another option for instances when the name of the person who had raised the idea or concern was unknown. Mary and Jim would develop a complete list of every idea or concern that did not have an owner attached. They would then post this list, with their responses to each and every item, on the main communication reader board.

Jim and Mary knew there were many contacts which they had not recorded. They would acknowledge this and encourage those who wished to come forward again. This time, they would record the idea or concern and close with the individual personally.

Action #2—Closure on Assigned Actions

Jim and Mary had settled on a two-pronged approach to address this issue. First, meeting leaders would receive additional training regarding conducting efficient meetings. In the future, if an action item were assigned during a meeting, the meeting leader would be held accountable for ensuring that the person who accepted the action item had the ability to complete the action as scheduled. The meeting leader was responsible for ensuring that closure happened and that the action item owner had the available time to properly close the action in a timely manner.

The second part of this action focused on the individual employee and his or her understanding that if an action item was accepted, there would be closure in a timely manner. Just as with the meeting leaders, the employees would be expected to step forward and say whether they had the correct skills, the right competency, and the sufficient time to close the action item. When accepting action items, employees should understand that there was ownership for complete, timely closure.

Day-to-Day Operations

Well documented, communicated, and understood ground rules and methods for day-to-day operations were clearly absent within the factory. Yet, having those established ground rules and methods in place was necessary to achieve the desired results.

As Jim, Mary, and the others looked over the list of rules and methods, they agreed that the list was basically a restatement of many of the previously noted actions, with a few additions.

One of the keys to getting the entire factory focused on the right priorities and the right goals was to ensure that all of the factory's employees knew what was expected of them on a daily basis. The workforce needed to know exactly what was required from them, individually and collectively, if the goals of the factory as a whole were to be met.

Management needed to clearly define goals for safety, quality, and output, and then document and communicate those goals. Finally, those goals needed to be interpreted for each and every employee on a daily basis. Each individual employee needed to have a clear understanding of what needed to be done. Further, employees should understand the exact priorities associated with each and every task that they performed.

Once the goals for the factory and for every worker within the factory were defined, there needed to be an easy way for each employee and each team of employees to gain access to their ongoing performance against the shift goals. The factory workforce should know that after one hour of production, they were either on target, ahead of target, or behind target. That same process should happen every hour, on the hour, throughout the work period.

In that way, each employee or team of employees would have time to make the necessary adjustments to ensure that the day's goals were met. If they needed to ask for help to bring output or quality back on track to meet the goals for that day, they would have time to seek that help.

Action #1—Quality Control

Since the laser/cut machine was critical to factory success, the group developed a plan that would maximize utilization of that piece of equipment without sacrificing quality. Patricia suggested that they name the plan the L/C Zero Downtime Plan. As part of this plan, operators and equipment maintenance technicians would be charged with ensuring that the laser/cut machine never stopped running during a scheduled work period.

The supervisors worked together to develop operator and equipment maintenance technician break and lunch coverage plans. All preventative maintenance was moved to off-shift hours, and all unscheduled downtime would now be addressed immediately, by no less than two qualified technicians. The goal for that piece of equipment was to achieve the highest possible output every shift while maintaining quality.

"Can anyone suggest what should be done if the laser/cut machine's output for the day is below goal?" Jim asked the supervisors.

Jerry looked thoughtful, then shrugged and said, "How about adding one hour of lost output recovery time for only the laser/cut machine immediately following the work period?"

Patricia was nodding. "If output is still below goal, we could also add one hour of overtime immediately before the next scheduled shift."

"And if output for the week is below goal," Jerry added, "an overtime Saturday could be added to help recover lost output."

Jim agreed and added the ideas to the flipchart. Everyone in the room knew that product quality issues were adding many extra hours of work to the factory. Once a customer reported a problem, there were often thousands of pieces of bad product inside the factory, or in the warehouse awaiting shipment.

With the agreement of quality manager Pat Peters, who had joined the meeting for this discussion, they designed what they called the Quality First effort. This effort focused on making quality a priority for everyone in the factory. If an operator or equipment maintenance technician identified a quality issue, they were to stop and immediately notify either Patricia or Darin.

Jim charged Patricia and Darin to bring the right resources together to address this issue immediately. If there were equipment issues, Mary and the appropriate members of her team would stop what they were doing and immediately respond. If there were suspected product or process issues, Mary or another appropriate engineering manager would be contacted. If an engineering manager was contacted, that manager was responsible for immediately assuming ownership for the issue. They owned bringing the right technical resources together to begin immediate quality issue containment, and then long-term resolution activities. As the quality manager, Pat Peters agreed to actively participate in all of the investigations associated with suspected quality issues.

To help facilitate a more positive environment, the supervisors decided to offer a Quality Bounty to any operator or equipment maintenance technician who identified and started actions toward addressing any valid quality problem. They developed a set of boundary conditions to ensure consistency in making bounty awards. The bounty award process would be a temporary program and would serve to publicize the importance of quality. Patricia accepted ownership for the Quality Bounty program.

Action #2—Management of Priority Changes

Jim realized that simply establishing a more effective method for the communication of priorities and priority changes would not address the problem of ever-changing priorities. Having the factory start with one set of priorities, and then changing that set of priorities almost immediately, was a problem.

"One thing Mary and I realized in our planning discussion," Jim said, "was that a great deal of output is being lost to the extra hours spent tearing down the existing work orders and then setting up for new work orders. There are also a number of quality issues that have been directly linked to the current practices. A number of employees have been frustrated with having to spend significant amounts of time restarting after they just started.

"Although the nature of the work performed in the factory does require a certain amount of flexibility, the costs associated with the constant fits and jerks need to be addressed. Does anyone have any ideas?"

The supervisors remained quiet for a minute, and then Devon spoke up. "I would suggest establishing a set of criteria to allow for more informed change decisions. Of course, we can't eliminate priority changes completely."

"That's right, Devon," said Jim, scribbling on the flipchart. "The goal is to make sounder, more informed business decisions."

The other supervisors chimed in and proposed that the change criteria become part of a new change process. This new change process established a method for work order changes within the factory. Simply put, anyone could ask to have the work order that was currently being processed changed. As part of that request, supervisors should consider the reason for the request, the amount of time required, and the amount of lost output (quantified into actual production dollar costs) that would result from the change-over.

If the reason for the requested change outweighed the costs, the change would be made within 30 minutes. The extra 30 minutes would allow work orders that were almost completed to be finished. The change-over plan would include a rolling set-up change as the pipeline cleared.

After they had sketched out a change plan, Jim said, "I want to emphasize one more time that the purpose of the process is not to limit the number of changes. Instead, we just want to ensure that there is business justification for any changes. I'd like to add that if a change that interrupts current factory processing can't be justified, this process should still allow for the work order in question to be moved forward on the next-to-be processed schedule of work orders."

Jim decided to personally spearhead the efforts associated with this proposal. He planned to partner with Phillip, the production control manager, on that effort. Jim's goal was to have a modified version of the process in place and working within one week. The final version would take several weeks to implement.

Action #3—Break Coverage Planning

One of the clear messages that Mary and Jim had received was that employees were confused about priorities and about the value they each personally brought to Amber Rose. Therefore, management needed to ensure that ground rules were in place regarding break and lunch coverage at critical locations throughout the factory. The supervisors had agreed that this problem needed to be addressed. Together, they developed a simple set of rules that would allow first the supervisors, and later the individual employees, to determine which equipment and work areas required coverage.

The rules were simple. Developing the data to use with the rules would take some time, however.

The Rules

•	If a piece of equipment or a work area has the ability to produce 1.5 times the output of the station that is immediately before it, coverage is not required for breaks and lunches. Coverage requirements for absences of longer than 30 minutes are to be determined on a case-by-case basis.

•	Should any piece of equipment or any work area be down for longer than one hour due to unexpected and/or unplanned circumstances, 100% coverage will be maintained until the output of that equipment or work area is current to targeted output for that shift. The exception is when the station immediately before the station in question, also known as the feeding station or the upstream station, is also unexpectedly not producing output.

• Any time the equipment, or the work area that a piece of equipment or other work area provides work to – also known as the downstream or fed equipment or work area – is unable to process work, or gets backed up with more than one-half of one shift's worth of work in inventory queue, there is no need for break and lunch coverage for that equipment or work area. This remains true until the downstream station has worked the inventory in queue down to less than two hours of process time.

The data to be used was a comprehensive set of output capability information for each and every piece of equipment and work area within the factory. Only after collecting that data and understanding which pieces of equipment had the lowest output could a comprehensive break and lunch coverage plan be developed. The lowest output equipment and work area(s) would be staffed 100% of the time every shift. That included during meetings, breaks, and lunches. Further, scheduled maintenance rules would be established to ensure that the equipment or work areas in question were truly producing work 100% of the scheduled time during a work period. This was accomplished by conducting the preventative maintenance for those stations with lowest output off-shift to eliminate all impacts to output.

Action #4—Communication of Products and Priorities

The first step in the communication of priorities and priority changes would be accomplished through the implementation of the communication reader boards. However, there were two remaining gaps.

The first gap in communication was associated with the importance of the products that were actually being produced in the factory. Only if the factory employees were able to understand what was being built, the ultimate use of the product that was being built, and the special significance of a particular work order, could they then understand the true value of the work they performed.

Jim proposed that he assume ownership for establishing a communication process to introduce new products to the factory's employees. He would work with Mary and her engineers to develop simple product communication overviews. In some cases, that might include bringing in guest speakers, or it might only involve flyers or posters that would be placed on the communication reader boards. There would be rare cases when engineers could also bring samples of the finished products to the factory for the employees to see.

The second gap in communication was associated with the significance of the various tasks that individual employees performed. Only after an understanding of this significance was clearly established could an individual employee make the right decisions regarding exactly what tasks to perform and at what time.

Mary assumed leadership of this effort. She committed to have her engineers develop a simple set of presentations that would focus on the "added value" that each work area within the factory provided to the products that were built. They would include that information as part of the preparation for all future products. Mary committed to a one-week turn-around on the first copies of the information. She explained that all of the data and details were already part of the information that her engineers had developed in preparation for new products entering the factory. However, they had never shared that information with the factory workforce.

General Operational Rules and Methods

The required actions to fill this gap would start with the development of a complete list of all of the other actions. Additional rules and methods could then be added to complete a more comprehensive list. Jim and Mary hoped to develop a comprehensive list that could become a part of the factory's daily operating methods. In addition to all of the specifically defined actions, this list included the following two action steps.

Action #5—Rules that We Work By

• Every shift will start on time. We are disciplined in our expectation that there are no exceptions to this rule.

• Every shift will end on time. We are just as disciplined in our adherence to this rule as we are to our start rule.

• Every piece of critical equipment and every critical work area will be staffed 100% of the time during every shift. Coverage for key stations will be provided during breaks and lunches, start-of-shift communication meetings, training sessions, and during all other events which may remove the operators and equipment maintenance technicians from the critical stations.

• Every shift ends with a complete set-up for the next shift. It is the responsibility of each shift to ensure that the next shift will be even better than the shift that has just been completed.

• Break and lunch schedules will be created and posted on the factory communication reader board. 100% coverage will be maintained at all key stations.

• We all own making ongoing performance status visible. Every employee will know their performance throughout the work period. Every employee will do real-time tracking of performance on at-station tracking sheets. Every work area will do real-time tracking using the communication reader board for that area. Every shift will do real-time tracking using the communication reader board for the factory.

Action #6—Methods that We Follow

•   We will always have the right staffing in the right place at the right time. We understand the staffing requirements for all equipment and work areas. We will ensure that equipment and work areas that constrict overall factory output receive continual focus and are staffed at all times. We will ensure that as the situation changes throughout the work period, trained and skilled staffing is considered, and appropriate changes will be made in a timely manner.

•   Factory cleanliness will be a matter of daily routine, including housekeeping procedures, expectations, checklists, and audits. Factory cleanliness is a matter of pride within the factory.

Action #7—Equipment Downtime Tracking Methodology

The meeting attendees agreed that equipment downtime practices must be changed. Work was initiated to reduce the time required to generate an impromptu equipment downtime report. However, the computer information department was unable to commit to anything less than six months to provide the desired reduction.

As an interim step, Mary would locate an old time clock and some four-inch by six-inch note cards. Operators who had equipment issues would immediately note the problem on the card and punch it down with the time clock. The card was then placed in a rack that would be installed above the time clock. The equipment technicians were expected to respond to all unscheduled equipment downtime within five minutes. If a higher priority needed to be addressed, the technician notified the operator (who then went to another station to help support its operation) and the equipment supervisor. The location of the priority and the expected time to start the response had to be reported.

Once the equipment was repaired, the equipment maintenance technician punched it up with the time clock and then notified both the operator and the equipment supervisor of the status. The equipment supervisor was expected to communicate on an ongoing basis with the production supervisors. All downtime cards would be tracked and trended to provide a better understanding and to help formally address unscheduled downtime issues.

Action #8—Factory Cleanliness and Housekeeping

The supervisors agreed that the factory needed to be cleaned up. The lost bolt incident had been embarrassing for the operators and the supervisors alike. Being too busy to put tools away, to complete the paperwork associated with a job, or to maintain an orderly work area were all examples of very poor work practices.

The production supervisors acknowledged that there was considerable lost output associated with the extra time it took the critical station operators to find everything they needed to do their work. They also acknowledged that there had been several people-related quality incidents associated with "lost" process changes that had not been properly followed. Later investigation had revealed that those changes were frequently buried in the paperwork and assorted "stuff" located at some work areas.

There was agreement to make factory cleanliness a matter of the daily routine within the factory. Factory cleanliness would become an expectation of everyone. The supervisors would simply remind the operators and equipment maintenance technicians to pick up after themselves. It might take a few weeks, but they would get everything cleaned up and would provide ongoing housekeeping reminders to keep it clean.

"I'll say it again," Darin said after Jim described the cleanliness issue. "These are too simple. Most of the actions we've listed are part of our everyday jobs – things we should have been doing all along. Are you sure we've identified the right problems? Have we really done a thorough enough job of identifying the actions we need to take to improve the factory's performance?"

"Darin, why do you think we named this set of actions Winning Basics?" Jim asked. "Of course most of the items we've listed are actions we should have been taking. The plain and simple truth is that we lost the formula for success. We need to get back to the Winning Basics that would make any manufacturer successful. We don't need a program-of-the-month to fix our problems. We need to capture the actions that are core to successful manufacturing operations and make those a part of the way we conduct our business. Do you agree?"

Darin nodded. "I do. It's just that I've been thinking how basic these actions really are. I can't believe it took all of us the majority of the day to create a plan of action that should have been in place all this time anyway." He threw his hands up in the air in bewilderment. "Where did we go wrong?"

"I don't think it's a question of where we went wrong," Jim said, trying to reassure him. "We just need to learn from this experience. We need to make sure that once we're performing the basics well, we never slip back into our old habits. We need to make sure that the next time we meet, we're talking about how to become the best at what we do. We don't want to stop with just getting the basics down. There's room for huge improvement after we have that done. Don't you agree?"

Darin nodded, and there were murmurs of agreement from everyone.

"Okay, then let's get back to the task at hand," Jim directed.

Employee Training and Development

Knowing the status of employee training and cross-training in the factory would have significantly reduced the time and money required to fill voids in the factory's ability to properly staff some stations and work areas. Having the right training in place would have also potentially allowed those trained employees to uncover issues and problems, and even possibly solve those problems.

Action #1—Factory Training Plan

The supervisors agreed that there were many training gaps within the factory. From an operational point of view, there were both equipment and work areas where no one had been trained. In other cases, there were not enough operators trained to meet the need. In still other cases, the training was inadequate to meet the needs of the operation. Finally, in some cases there was no identified training to support newly requested tasks. This was particularly common in the case of technical inspections.

On the technical side, the equipment maintenance supervisors complained about the total lack of training planning. Yet, there were specialized training needs. In many cases, the technicians were being asked to perform highly specialized tasks without that training. In other cases, when training had been requested, there was no training available to support the request. Sending technicians to equipment manufacturer-sponsored classes was next to impossible. Very little training was offered to support the equipment and technologies at Amber Rose Industries. Even when training was available, the cost would be a strain on the budget.

There needed to be a comprehensive training plan for the factory, one that would ensure that every station had the required number of trained employees. Such a plan needed to include both operators and equipment maintenance technicians. The Factory Training Plan would focus first on ensuring that the right skills and competencies were in place to meet the factory's current needs.

Once current needs were fully covered, the plan would look to the future. As products, processes, and equipment became more complex, the plan would include training and development in anticipation of that increase in complexity.

Action #2—Training Materials

Once a training plan was in place, the next challenge was to ensure that the correct training materials were available. They had already run into a recent situation in which the equipment vendor had made a commitment to provide them with both the training and the training materials but failed to deliver.

The supervisors decided to follow two specific courses of action in support of this action item. First, after the Factory Training Plan was created, they wanted to go line-item by line-item and verify that materials existed to support the plan. Whenever they found that materials were in existence, they would verify that the materials were in fact in use in the factory. Whenever they identified a lack of training materials, they would focus their efforts on buying or developing those materials.

Action #3—Employee Training and Development Plans

Individual Employee Training and Development Plans would be helpful in aligning individual employee training with the current and future needs of the factory.

Just as there was a need to develop a Factory Employee Training Plan, each employee needed an individual training and development plan. The initial pieces of the Individual Employee Training and Development Plans would be found on the Factory Training Plan. Those items would be carried directly over to the appropriate employee's own training plan.

In addition, training would be placed on an employee's plan in anticipation of future needs. For example, if the supervisors knew that an employee was going to be promoted, or that an employee was planning to leave ARI, they could place the required training on the plan of an employee who was remaining. In that way, once an employee left, there could be a fully trained employee ready to assume the tasks of the employee who had just left.

General training that was delivered to all employees would be placed on the Individual Employee Training and Development Plan for every factory employee.

As they discussed this last action item, Jim sensed that the supervisors were finally beginning to see the potential for eliminating many of the problems that they had been facing on a daily basis.

"Jim, this is a great idea," Patricia commented. "But it's going to cost us a lot of operator time."

"That's right," Darin agreed.

"What do you mean?" Jim asked.

"If everyone has a training and development plan, everyone will be getting trained," Patricia explained. "Who's going to be left to run the factory?"

Jim nodded thoughtfully. "Let's talk about that. We said that every factory employee would have a training and development plan. We didn't say that every employee would be in training all the time. Right?"

"That's right," said Patricia hesitantly. "But I don't understand where you're going with this."

"It's going to require some excellent planning on the part of all of you, and more importantly, on the part of your teams," Jim replied. "You'll need to ensure that we're intelligently prioritizing and executing training in the factory. My expectation is that training and development will never negatively impact the output or the quality of the work performed in the factory. You need to know what training needs to be completed and develop a plan to execute and monitor that training to ensure that it occurs as planned."

Patricia opened her mouth to object, but Jim quickly pressed on.

"It won't be easy, but it can be done. Certainly we need to place a focused effort on making it happen. If we don't successfully meet our training needs, we can't meet our output needs."

Patricia paused for a moment to absorb Jim's words, then nodded. "Okay. We just need to make sure we're doing an outstanding job of planning and executing our training."

The final point of discussion had to be the *how* and *when* of communicating the Winning Basics information to the entire workforce. Suggestions from the supervisors ranged all over the map.

"I don't think anything formal needs to be said," Devon insisted. "Just initiate the actions we've listed, and let's not waste time with any more meetings."

"I disagree," said Patricia, shaking her head. "Haven't we been saying over and over how important communication is? I don't think anything should be started until every employee knows exactly what's going on. We could give a presentation, including all the actions and supporting information we've been talking about."

After ten minutes of back-and-forth discussion, Jim said, "Can I make a suggestion?"

Everyone became silent, and all eyes turned in his direction.

"Mary and I will show up at the all-hands, start-of-shift meeting tomorrow morning. Let us have about three minutes to make a high-level, informational statement. I think we can give everyone a feel for the urgency of this endeavor and provide enough detail to get things kicked off.

"We will then look to each of you to spend fifteen minutes, sometime during tomorrow's shift, with each work team. We'll provide each of you with a basic checklist of information to be covered during your fifteen minutes. We'll also include a date, time, and place for a more formal communication meeting that we'll hold with everyone. We'll repeat the process when the back-end shifts report to work later this week. How does that sound?"

Patricia was shaking her head even before he finished. "I think we need to hold the formal meeting before we do anything."

Jim thought for a moment. "You know, Patricia, if we weren't in the position of having to provide results this week, I would be in total agreement. But we just don't have the time to prepare everything we'd need for a formal meeting. We don't have a room, and we haven't informed the employees that there will be a meeting. It would take at least one more day to pull that meeting together. That would mean losing three of the five days this week, and we just plain don't have the luxury of taking that amount of time. So while I agree with you in principle, in reality we don't have many options. This is a risk. If we all work together and handle it correctly, I don't think it'll be a problem."

After a few more comments, the group agreed with Jim's assessment. They then went on to discuss exactly how they would handle unexpected problems and issues. The key message that Jim and Mary gave everyone was that they would be there immediately if and when there was a need for support of any kind.

They also discussed the information they felt the employees would want immediately:

- What are the changes to be made?
- Why are these changes being made?
- What are the expected results to be achieved?
- When will the changes take place?
- What does it mean to each individual employee?

Jim gave the supervisors some of the basic answers to the questions they had identified.

"I'll publish a comprehensive list of answers before the next shift starts," he concluded. "I'll also commit to answering all the listed questions as part of the information Mary and I will be sharing with the employees at the start of the next shift."

With that, the meeting ended. Looking around the room, Jim saw haggard expressions and heavy eyelids. It was late, and it had been a very long day for all of them. He felt sure that everyone was as hungry and tired as he was.

"Tomorrow is the day that we get this all started," Jim said as he shuffled his papers into a pile. "Get a good night's sleep. We have a lot of work to do. Thank you all for the great job you did today."

After a round of goodbyes and pats on the back, everyone slowly filed out of the conference room. As they left, several thanked Jim and Mary for their leadership during the meeting.

Jim left the plant at 10:00 that night. As he drove home, he couldn't help but ask himself if he had really made the right decision. While every problem they had identified was real, he had committed to an aggressive timeline. Was it possible to achieve implementation by the time Brian would be expecting results? Would Brian even let them finish the presentations to the employees before he fired them?

He also wondered if Mary would be there tomorrow. She had changed her mind so many times during the day that Jim had lost count. Two of her supervisors had approached Jim after the planning meeting to ask what Jim was going to do about her negative attitude. They both said that they found her to be a "real downer."

Jim's thoughts drifted back to his decision to come to work for Amber Rose Industries. He had been employed by a manufacturer in an entirely different field before moving to Amber Rose. When he had given his employer notice that he was leaving, there had been a quick counter-offer that included a new, higher-level position and a significant raise. His former boss had also told him that he was targeted to be groomed for a top-level senior management position in the future. Finally, his boss had warned him to be careful at Amber Rose.

If he had only known how careful I needed to be, Jim said to himself.

After a 30-minute drive, he pulled into his driveway. He and his wife had purchased this home only two years ago, yet Jim couldn't imagine living anywhere else.

Tanya, his wife of four years, was waiting with their son Andy in her arms as Jim walked through the door. He had called and given her a brief summary of the day's excitement before he had left for home, and now she was ready to hear the whole story. Even though she had met Brian Jones only once, she probably knew him better than anyone else who worked at Amber Rose Industries. Jim had frequently told her about Brian's outrageous behavior. Tanya had encouraged Jim to find another job, and Brian had been making that look more and more like a possibility.

Andy, who had just celebrated his first birthday, started laughing as Jim took him from Tanya's arms and hoisted him into the air.

This is what makes it all worthwhile, Jim thought. He couldn't contain the smile that came to his face whenever he held his son.

Later, after putting Andy to bed, Jim told Tanya all about his day.

She encouraged Jim to give his two-weeks notice first thing the following morning. "You don't need this," she reminded him as they prepared for bed. "Maybe you can return to SDV and pick up where you left off with them. I'll bet they'd re-hire you in a minute and would be happy to have you back."

"I'm not going back to SDV," Jim said firmly as he changed into his pajamas. "I'll be meeting with Mary and the supervisors from eight until noon tomorrow. Then I'll meet with Brian after lunch."

Tanya looked dubious. "It's your decision," she said with a shrug. "I just don't understand why you're doing this to yourself."

"I really can't explain it either," a tired Jim said as he fell into bed. It took him less than a minute to drift off to sleep.

Chapter 9
First Week's Results

Results from the first week were shocking. Mary and Jim found more problems than they could have ever imagined. These were the types of problems that might take months to solve—yet they only had hours. With some ingenuity and luck, they had increased factory output by 23%, and there were no reported quality issues.

Training for the Paste Pre-Mix Machine

While participating in one of the new start-of-shift standup meetings, Mary discovered that there was still no one with formal training to operate the new mixer on the paste dispenser. Training materials were still not available. The manufacturer of the paste dispenser had promised to provide a representative to conduct the training, but that person had gotten sick. No one had reported this problem to either Jim or Mary. Though this had been called out as a stand-alone action in the plan, it had not been implemented.

When she asked the supervisors about this, they told her that with all of the problems involved just in getting the equipment to dispense paste, there hadn't been time to worry about training.

Mary contacted the paste dispenser manufacturer about the problem. While they could provide the training materials, there was no one available to provide training for at least two more weeks. The manufacturer pointed out that while the model 2460 looked much different, the controls were in exactly the same spot as the model 1960, which this dispenser had replaced. The training materials were overnight expressed to Mary.

Mary next pulled together a small group of paste pre-mix machine equipment maintenance technicians and the designated operators to determine what they needed and how to handle it. John Peelman, one of the equipment maintenance technicians, reminded Mary that both he and Juan Rodriguez had been through the entire paste dispenser training before bringing the equipment into the factory. They could provide the operational training if the materials were available.

Mary helped develop a plan to complete the operational training. John and Juan would move to the paste dispenser, ensuring that one of them was present at all times. In addition to their maintenance duties on the paste machine, they would become the "head operators" for a day. Until the training materials arrived, they would provide hands-on training. Once the training materials arrived, two operators would start training immediately. The balance would be trained once training for the first two had been completed.

Mary also shared the operating information that she had received during her phone calls with the paste manufacturer. John, Juan, and the operators agreed to a warm handoff plan, since the paste dispenser was limiting all other activities in the factory. In this process, there would always be a person running the paste dispenser from the moment a shift started until the entire shift ended. They also agreed to run overtime one hour extra after the end of each working shift and one hour prior to the start of the next working shift. They would continue this practice until a permanent plan could be developed and implemented.

John, Juan, and Mary also developed a paste dispenser troubleshooting checklist to help more effectively deal with unexpected equipment problems. Juan took ownership for creating and publishing the list, reviewing it with all of the equipment maintenance personnel and collecting completed troubleshooting checklists.

John and Juan would meet with Mary at the end of every shift to look for common equipment problems so they could focus on fixing the biggest downtime issues first.

Communication

All-Hands, Start-Of-Shift Meetings

The all-hands, start-of-shift meetings were going well. A few of Patricia's employees who had previously been able to just barely make it inside the building entrance by the time the shift started were having a little difficulty making it to the meeting on time. However, as the importance and benefits of the meeting became more obvious, there was a noticeable change in their tardiness. The meetings had ended up averaging about 12 minutes in length. The extra time was being used to answer employee questions and to ensure that station and break/lunch coverage assignments were clear to everyone.

Communication Reader Boards

The real-time reader boards had been installed and were of some help. However, getting the information posted on time was causing havoc. Often the supervisors argued over who was responsible for posting the updates and who actually *had* to post the updates. So far, the information was being posted, but it obviously came with a cost.

At-Station Tracking Sheets

The at-station tracking sheets met with a great deal of employee resistance. Employees complained that the sheets required too much time and that the information was not of any value. Some of the employees felt that their supervisors might start using the information punitively against them. In addition, there was concern that use of the tracking sheets was counter to the cleanliness and housekeeping efforts. According to the argument, all the tracking sheets accomplished was to add even more papers around the factory.

After many discussions between the supervisors and operators, they asked Jim to act as a mediator in resolving the conflict. Jim met with the operators and listened to their concerns. He got some informal data regarding exactly how many had tried the tracking sheets and how they felt. As those operators who had actually used the tracking sheets began to share their positive thoughts and feelings, the complaints of those who had not given the process a chance became less vocal.

Paul, one of the equipment operators who had initially been most outspoken against the tracking sheets, raised a hand. "Jim, after hearing Dave and Randy's feedback, I guess I'd be willing to give the tracking sheets another chance."

Jim looked around the conference table at the other operators and saw a few heads nodding.

"But what if they still don't work out?" asked Susan. "How long do we have to give this idea before we decide one way or the other?"

Jim thought about that for a moment. "I suggest that everyone use the process for one month. If, at the end of that month, you can show that it adds too much work or clutter, or that the supervisors are using the information against you in any way, request a follow-up meeting with me, and we'll decide what to do. Does that sound fair?"

The operators and supervisors nodded their agreement, although Susan still looked skeptical.

"Thank you all for sharing your concerns," Jim concluded, "and for being open to the interim plan we've developed. There will be more changes coming as we continue working to improve the factory's performance. I'd like to ask all of you to look for improvement opportunities and always be willing to share your questions and concerns with your supervisors."

Policies, Procedures, Guidelines & Expectations

There was nothing to report in this category. Jim had the management meetings scheduled for the following week, but there had been no changes during the first week.

Meeting Commitments

Jim was happy that they had removed the original set of actions associated with this category from the Winning Basics plan. Everyone was completely focused on achieving the basic day-to-day factory results. He was confident that the timing for an effort of this magnitude would have been wrong. He appreciated that there was a need for focused efforts on factory performance at this time and was confident that the efforts would be successful.

Jim hoped that at some point in the near future, he would be able to start working with the supervisors to begin developing actions that supported meeting commitments. In the short-term, however, he would continue to drive accountability and role-model meeting commitments in his day-to-day behavior.

Day-to-Day Operations

Break and Lunch Coverage

Providing non-stop coverage at all key stations was also creating issues. Many operators had grown accustomed to shutting down the factory completely, which allowed them to go on their breaks and lunches together. When they were asked to ensure that coverage was continuous at key locations, they had agreed. But when the time came and they found that they could not have breaks and lunches with their best friends, they had chosen to ignore their previous commitment and instead to go to lunch together. Not covering breaks and lunches had greatly impacted total factory output.

Jim and Mary worked with the supervisors and Jane Donaldson from Human Resources to develop a modification to the break guideline that allowed for more flexibility in break timing. With the new guideline, employees could take their breaks within designated break time windows. This allowed friends to go to lunch together while ensuring that there was coverage at critical locations.

Factory Cleanliness and Housekeeping

Cleaning the factory had turned into a major challenge. While it had looked like applying a little focused effort and spending just a little time would be the solution, it had become clear that this was going to be a major effort requiring sound leadership. During their newly established weekly meeting with the supervisors, Jim and Mary asked if a supervisor would be willing to form a working team that included operators and equipment maintenance technicians.

The team's charge would be to develop a complete housekeeping and factory appearance process. That included establishing the procedures and supporting paperwork and checklists. To the relief of his peers, Jerry offered to help coordinate the effort, which was also a pleasant surprise to Mary and Jim.

Product Change Control

The plan to control the number of changes within the factory met with much resistance outside the factory. Those in the production control department felt that Jim was tying their hands by not accepting any and all changes whenever they were requested. That resistance to change had been taken to Brian every day since Brian approved the action plan. True to his word, Brian had voiced his support for Mary, Jim, and the Winning Basics effort every time he was faced with the question.

Equipment Maintenance Process

The critical equipment preventative maintenance process was working well. The equipment maintenance technicians, eager to maximize output, found it easy to schedule the equipment work during non-production time. The overtime pay that the equipment technicians received for the extra off-hours work didn't hurt, either. This change had begun producing dividends immediately.

Unscheduled Equipment Downtime Management

The effort to make unscheduled equipment downtime visible on a real-time basis was a winner. Jerry reported that the equipment technicians were now made aware when the equipment they were responsible for maintaining was unexpectedly down. While they did not have data regarding lost output prior to the new downtime tracking process, they did have data now.

Jerry provided a complete set of performance graphs on a daily basis. He had broken the data down by piece of equipment, by response time (the amount of time it took an equipment maintenance technician to respond once a piece of equipment was logged down into the new system), by turn-around time (the amount of time that passed between reporting of a problem and the repair), and by callbacks (when a repair did not last due to misdiagnosis or incorrect repair). When that happened, someone had to return to correctly fix the original problem.

Jerry was proud to report that all of the issues he tracked and reported had improved on a daily basis since he had started tracking and reporting the results.

Employee Training and Development

Factory Training Plan

The Factory Training Plan had not been posted in the factory by the end of the first week. The supervisors indicated that they had simply been too busy to get the plan information collected and posted inside the factory.

Jim worried that this might be one more example of the supervisors making and not meeting commitments. They had not followed through as committed, and no one had approached either Mary or Jim with an update. Nor were there any requests for help.

Rather than letting this action plan item remain incomplete, Jim asked if some of the operators, equipment technicians, and supervisors would be interested in creating the training plan while having pizza with him after work the following Thursday. He told them they would be paid overtime and that the pizza would be his way of saying thanks for helping. So many people stepped forward to help that Jim had to use a lottery process to narrow the number down to a size that was appropriate for the tasks that were involved in developing the plan.

After the names were selected and they found that theirs were not on the list, several operators and two equipment maintenance technicians approached Jim and asked if there was a way that they could attend and help without overtime pay or pizza.

"Getting the training plan completed is very important," said Dave, who had made himself spokesperson. "It'll make our jobs easier, and we just want to help."

Jim was pleased by their enthusiasm, but he would simply have too many people on one project if they participated. "I'm sorry, Dave, but I really do have enough people on this. Would you be willing to help address other open action plan items?"

"Sure," said Dave. "I think we all would." The rest indicated that they would be glad to help, and Jim jotted down their names.

"There will be more than enough work for everyone to do before the action plan is fully implemented," Jim assured them. "I'll need a few days to find out what other action plan items are behind schedule, but I'll inform you as soon as I know."

This was one commitment that Jim would make sure he carried out.

Chapter 10
Second Week's Results

What a relief! Jim thought as he looked over the figures for the second week.

To his surprise, after the first week's adjustments had been made, factory output had gone up by another 50%. To meet their commitment to Brian, Jim, Mary, and the factory team only needed to achieve 33% improvement in the last week of the month.

He was beginning to see the opportunity to more than double factory output again by building on the recovery action plan efforts. The workforce had been asking how they had done so far. People were obviously excited when they saw that their goals had been met. When touring the factory floor, operators and maintenance personnel had begun to stop Jim and Mary. Sometimes they would ask about new products or provide an idea for a way to perform an operation more effectively. People wanted to be involved.

Jim had also suggested to Mary that they schedule daily, ten-minute one-on-one meetings during breaks. Mary had been enthusiastic, and they had both enjoyed the opportunity. If there was business to discuss, he and Mary spent the time discussing that business. If not, they spent the time getting to know each other, which included many stories about Jim's new baby.

One day as they were discussing the latest challenge—a proposal from the workforce to move a piece of equipment to improve efficiency—Mary looked at Jim with a smile and remarked, "What kind of monster have we created?"

Another surprise was Jerry. Ever since the meeting when the action plan had been developed, he had stepped forward as a true leader within his peer group. More than once, supervisors had mentioned the coaching and support Jerry had provided around action plan items. Jerry was becoming a positive leader within the organization.

Communication

All-Hands, Start-of-Shift Meetings

A few glitches had occurred in the all-hands, start-of-shift meetings during the second week. While there were several small missteps, one of the biggest glitches involved supervisor leadership of the meeting. The supervisors had agreed to rotate primary ownership for the meeting among their peer group. That ownership included being responsible for preparing the update and informational materials to be presented at the meeting.

On Tuesday, all of the supervisors, operators, and equipment maintenance technicians had gathered for the meeting. When the meeting was ready to start, however, no one was prepared to take the leadership role.

Apparently, the supervisors had taken their own individual notes regarding exactly when they would each take the leader role. A master schedule had not been published. Every supervisor had expected another supervisor to take the lead for the meeting, and no one stepped forward.

After a few awkward moments, Jerry jumped in and assumed the meeting leadership role. Because he was not prepared, the meeting did not include all of the usual details. Jerry did commit to having the information pulled together and the details posted on the communication reader board immediately following the start-of-shift meeting.

Jerry had a complete roll-up of the leadership schedule published to all of the supervisors by mid-shift that day.

Communication Reader Boards

The supervisors continued to have problems posting the right information on the main factory communication reader board. As a short-term action, Darin had assumed full ownership of the issue.

The operators and technicians had begun to use the board as their primary source of factory status information. Darin realized that the right behavior was occurring, and he really appreciated the enthusiasm and team spirit that was beginning to develop. Operators were jumping in and offering to help their peers when they were behind on meeting shift output. He had even seen Mary's equipment maintenance technicians covering operator breaks when there were no equipment maintenance issues. He wanted to reinforce those behaviors.

Jim was seeing the beginnings of the same behaviors. He also was beginning to see a couple of the supervisors assume stronger leadership roles within their peer group.

At-Station Tracking Sheets

At-station tracking sheets were still not an overwhelming success. The operators continued to feel resentful that they were required to complete the tracking sheets. Many saw this as information that others owed to them, and they complained that taking the two or three minutes each hour to log the numbers was, in fact, limiting output.

The operators who had initially started using the sheets remained enthusiastic about them. They liked being able to see exactly where they were during the shift. They also liked having the supervisors come by their work areas periodically to see how they were doing. When the supervisors visited them, there was always a positive word to start the visit. Even better, when they were on track or ahead of schedule, the supervisors provided some very positive feedback—which felt good. When they were behind, the supervisors took the time to coach them in ways to recover lost output.

Policies, Procedures, Guidelines & Expectations
The first of the management meetings regarding policies and guidelines had gone very well. Even Brian had attended and actively participated. One manager had failed to attend, and Brian had immediately contacted her and directed her to attend a make-up session with Brian and Jane Donaldson.

Self-Discipline and Shared Ownership
Operators and equipment maintenance technicians were beginning to see that their ideas for improving the factory could have positive effects on the factory's performance. They had begun to identify issues, and they wanted to fix those issues. Unfortunately, since the workforce had previously not been asked to help make improvements, there was a lack of training associated with good problem-solving processes. Factory employees were stepping forward and trying to solve the problems, but they simply were not prepared. As a result, the quality of the problem-solving was leading to the implementation of some bad solutions.

In one case, a decision within a small work group to change their break coverage practices caused one of the factory's limiting stations to run out of work.

The employees had established a rotation plan that allowed everyone to have breaks and lunches. They had examined the flow of work into their workstation during the course of two work shifts. Using the data from those two shifts, they had determined that there was a decrease in workflow at precisely 11:30 a.m. every shift. They therefore decided to use that to their advantage and left only one person in the factory from 11:30 a.m. to noon.

They were lucky the first shift after the plan was implemented, and everything worked as planned. However, during the next shift, the rest of the work area team returned from their lunch to find that the one remaining operator had over 100 pre-assemblies waiting to be processed. They had over one full shift of work piled up and knew that it would take almost two shifts to work off the excess inventory while still meeting normal workflow.

Upon further investigation, they found that the two data points they were using for their problem-solving occurred when one of the pieces of equipment that fed work to them was down to allow annual preventative maintenance to be performed. The extra 100 pre-assemblies represented the excess work that had backed up during that preventative maintenance. With the feeding area equipment now functioning, they had to go back to the previous break and lunch schedule to keep up with the inflow of work.

Management's challenge was to continue to nurture that employee willingness to be involved while providing both training and real-time coaching on good problem-solving methods.

Day-to-Day Operations

Factory Quality

There had been only one reported quality issue during the week. The issue appeared to have resulted from an operational error by one of the operators at the flying backlash machine during the temporary inspection process. However, with the new quality investigation process in place, the engineering department had determined that the problem occurred because of pressure changes that had been made for the experiment. Those changes had caused the earlier production problems.

A permanent solution was in place for the next shift. Prior to the Winning Basics effort, the process of developing and implementing a solution would have taken at least one full week. With the focus on quality across the factory, the right resources were immediately available to make the required changes.

Product Change Control

Generally, employees had accepted the process for making changes to work orders that were in process within the factory. However, the production control department still occasionally attempted to make changes without utilizing the process. Due in large part to Brian's continued support, they had stopped taking every desired change to him. In fact, they were now trying to work on a process that allowed the production control department to effectively prioritize work in the factory while minimizing the impact of the constant changes.

Factory Cleanliness and Housekeeping

Jerry's factory cleanliness and housekeeping team had held its first meeting. The team members had requested that they be allowed to meet for 45 minutes twice a week until some of the major challenges were addressed.

After examining the options, Jim countered the twice-weekly meetings proposal with a one-and-a-half hour, once per week meeting proposal. He also asked that the meeting start 30 minutes before the end of the shift and that the members work one hour of overtime to hold their meeting. Two members dropped off the team due to personal conflicts, and three other people volunteered to join.

The team developed some basic checklists during the first meeting and asked to have every person take five minutes during the first hour of the shift to clean up the work area. They also proposed starting a campaign called Keep our Factory Clean. The proposal was simple: Every day, people were asked to look for items that did not belong in the factory and remove them to a holding area. Members of the cleanliness and housekeeping team then sorted those items as time allowed.

Unscheduled Equipment Downtime Management

Equipment downtime indicators continued to improve. Jerry had started posting the daily and weekly equipment downtime graphs on the factory communication board. He also ensured that the results were discussed at the stand-up start of shift meetings. He continued to make sure individual equipment maintenance technicians were aware of the results associated with their specific pieces of equipment. If there was a trend toward slow turnaround time or an unusually high number of callbacks relative to the other equipment maintenance technicians, the supervisors offered to provide extra training and any other support that the technicians requested.

One of the equipment maintenance technicians contacted Mary with a concern that his supervisor would be using the equipment downtime information to punish him. While he liked to see the data, he was worried that his numbers were not as good as the numbers of his peers. Mary responded that he was correct; he had almost 100% callbacks on equipment that he repaired. She was able to work with the technician and his supervisor to develop a training plan to help address his inability to properly assess the causes of downtime. They also assigned a more senior technician, who was known for his excellent troubleshooting skills, as a coach. Finally, they gained agreement from the technician that he would ask for help when he was having trouble rather than guessing on the course of action to take.

Employee Training & Development

Factory Training Plan

The effort that was started after the first week to develop the Factory Training Plan had not had the time to gain traction. In fact, the pizza dinner meeting had resulted in more questions than answers. To some extent, Jim and the others had discussed what the final plan would look like.

While Jim had hoped to have something in place and working within a matter of a few weeks, he now realized that this was a much bigger issue than it had first seemed. Current training records did not exist. Many bits and pieces of information regarding training did exist, however. To really assess the current situation would require hours and hours of sifting through that information.

The training team, as Jim's pizza group started calling themselves, did start to develop an interim plan. Their goal was to identify the major training gaps and to begin training to fill those areas immediately.

A sub-team had been charged to begin developing a priority-training plan, and had committed to bring a first-pass list of factory priority-training needs to the next training team meeting. They would use their interim plan as a safety net for the factory until the work associated with the original plan was completed.

Chapter 11
The Improvement Continues

Just three short months after presenting the action plan to Brian, Jim couldn't believe the changes. During the past six weeks, the factory had met or exceeded the output schedule 100% of the time. Furthermore, there had not been a single quality issue during the last eight weeks. Jim was proud of this record. However, he was more proud of the changes that had taken place within the factory workforce.

During his most recent factory walk-through, Jim had observed several encouraging changes.

Factory Training Plan

A Factory Training Plan posted on the wall near the entrance to the factory reflected the names, dates, and planned training for every employee within the factory, including both operators and equipment maintenance technicians. Training that was deemed critical to factory success was in green letters. Training that met upcoming needs was in blue letters. Training that helped the employee grow, or met some long-term need for the business, was in purple.

The factory employees were keeping the training plan current by updating it regularly. The production and equipment maintenance supervisors had established a monthly meeting with the training team. The meeting agenda included a review of the training for the next month, time to agree on how to ensure that the training would always occur, and a plan to ensure that there was proper staffing so that training did not impact the factory's output performance.

Improvements in Output and Quality

Employees throughout the factory were recognizing opportunities to make improvements in output and quality. Employees would routinely stop Jim, Mary, or the supervisors to highlight potential issues they had identified. Even more encouraging, the operators and equipment maintenance technicians were now asking how they could help resolve the issues that they were identifying.

Employee Awareness and Attitude

Employees were now aware of the factory's status during their shift. Jim had adopted the practice of stopping to ask individual operators and equipment maintenance technicians how the factory was doing for that shift. He could ask for output status, quality status, and equipment status. When he began this practice during the first week following the implementation of the action plan, he had found that only about 50% of the employees could provide any kind of answer at all. Often, the answers they gave were incorrect.

Now, just three months later, approximately 80% of the employees could provide an answer, and almost all were correct. Even more encouraging to Jim was the fact that practically all those who did not know the answer were able to explain exactly how they could find the information that Jim was seeking. Jim's factory visits were now a pleasure.

Factory Cleanliness

Be Clutter-Free had become the final slogan adopted by Jerry and his team, and the factory truly reflected that slogan. The locations for everything were clearly identified and labeled. Anything that was not needed had been removed. Jim had been shocked by the request for two big dumpsters to haul off the trash that was being thrown out. They had filled both of the dumpsters to the top!

Work Order Changes

The work order change process had now been formalized. After a few minor corrections to the process, it had actually become one of Amber Rose's strengths. Now, when a change occurred and there was a delivery date commitment to a customer, that delivery date was met.

Employee Expectations

Finally, one of the biggest issues during the first 90 days had been establishing and communicating employee expectations. Manager and supervisor attendance and participation at all meetings had been good. However, there had been several breakdowns in the process.

Two supervisors had taken the information from the first expectations meeting and presented it to their operators and technicians. The technicians, in particular, had been upset by the wording of expectations associated with the attendance guideline. Human Resources modified the wording during their review of the management meeting recommendations, but the employees had already seen the initial meeting output.

Three particularly angry technicians had marched into Jane Donaldson's office without an appointment, threatening to quit if she didn't take care of the managers. Jane got the technicians to agree to meet with Mary and Jim, and things were resolved. It took an entire afternoon with all six people involved to address the concerns.

After the technicians had returned to their jobs, Jim and Mary contacted the two supervisors involved to better understand their reason for not following the agreed-upon plan. Both said they wanted to make sure their people received plenty of advance notice of the planned changes. They were shocked that the employees had overreacted, when all they were doing was offering them the courtesy of communicating early. Both supervisors said they understood the agreed-upon timeline, and they agreed not to violate that timeline in the future.

Out of all the challenges that the factory had met head-on during the past three months, one of the most unexpected surprises was Jerry. He had assumed a true leadership role within the factory. His peers would routinely seek his thoughts and ideas as part of problem-solving. Darin, too, had continued to step forward and assume greater leadership responsibilities.

Jim continued to meet with Mary on a daily basis, as well as weekly at the supervisor meeting. They had agreed to develop a Supervisor Training Plan, which would be created using the Factory Training Plan as the model.

Patricia had asked to help pull the information for the Supervisor Training Plan together. Jim was pleasantly surprised to see her grab the assignment and run with it. Just as she had taken on a bigger role toward the end of the Factory Training Plan effort, Patricia demonstrated that she really wanted to be a leader in this effort. Was there a new job in her future?

Brian's feedback had become more and more positive. He no longer attended the daily factory performance review meetings. Rather, he asked to be informed if there were problems that would impact customers. He also now conducted monthly factory performance review meetings. Rather than being concerned about the details of the factory's day-to-day performance, he began focusing on weekly and monthly factory performance trends. He also began to ask Jim more questions about future plans for the factory.

While Jim realized that the results were good for the short-term, he also knew that without a conscious, focused effort, it would be easy to slip back into the old ways. As he looked forward, Jim recognized that one of the next big opportunities for Amber Rose Industries would be to develop excellent problem-solving skills in every employee at the organization. These skills were critical for identifying the actual root causes of problems, and then identifying the real solutions to those root cause issues.

Chapter 12
Conclusion

Jim sat in his office at the end of another impressive week at the factory, reviewing the continuing improvements. As he had hoped, Amber Rose Industries had survived the recent crisis. Not only that, but factory performance had become much more consistent. As a result, customers were satisfied. In fact, Brian had mentioned to Jim just that day that he was hearing more and more positive feedback from existing customers, especially now that he was devoting more of his own time to sales and marketing.

Ultimately, Brian had been able to save "the big order." During their meetings, he seemed continually surprised by just how much business was available to ARI. He also seemed surprised by how simple the formula had become: Brian asked for the sale, and the factory delivered as committed!

Jim was proud of the success of Winning Basics. He and Mary often congratulated each other during their daily one-on-one meetings. Mary was clearly glad she had stayed on at ARI. The results they had achieved had required little significant spending and no additional staffing. Furthermore, no major changes to existing policies, procedures, and guidelines had been necessary. As a result of the efforts, the factory workforce was strong in its feedback. The workforce felt that they were being treated in a fairer, more consistent manner by management.

In retrospect, Jim realized that the actions they had taken were ridiculously simple. He couldn't help but agree with Darin's original observations about Winning Basics being a part of the fundamental day-to-day expectations in a manufacturing environment. It was the job of every manufacturing person to know the basics and to ensure that they were a part of the day-to-day operations.

Jim shuffled through the folder on his desk and took out the actions list for the Winning Basics plan. Looking through the list, he reflected on how well they had addressed each of the issues.

Communication

Jim had always considered himself a good communicator; he just hadn't realized the size of the information void in the factory. Most of the workforce had not even been aware that Amber Rose Industries was not meeting customer commitments. Once Jim realized exactly how big the communication gap had become, he immediately planned to invest even more in training the first-line supervisors. His goal was to ensure that all supervisors had as many communication tools as possible. Mary and Jim had already added communication to the expectations of the supervisors who worked directly for them.

The all-hands, start-of-shift meetings were an easily-implemented vehicle to ensure that there was a shared understanding of priorities by all personnel within the factory. Logistically, it was an easily managed meeting, and it helped to reinforce the importance of being in the factory at exactly the start of every shift to those supervisors and employees who had been lax in meeting that guideline.

The start-of-shift meeting was also the perfect opportunity for the supervisors to provide positive and reinforcing feedback to employees regarding the prior shift's performance. Recognizing good performance had not been a standard practice at ARI. This meeting provided a great opportunity to begin that practice, which was built into the meeting agenda. Positive feedback was also a benefit of the daily visits that the supervisors now made to every work area in the factory.

The communication reader boards were another easily initiated option to help ensure that communication occurred throughout the entire work period. The concern had been that if there was no tool or process to ensure ongoing communication, everything that could be gained through start-of-shift communication could immediately be lost.

The reader boards had remained a source of controversy among the supervisors until further refinements were made. However, they all agreed that the communication reader boards did serve a valuable purpose. Every employee had access to both priorities and current output information. There was also a new two-way communication vehicle available to anyone who chose to use it. Placing questions on the board was encouraged.

Policies, Procedures, Guidelines and Expectations

This portion of the plan was all about establishing a shared understanding of the company's policies, procedures, guidelines, and expectations. That shared understanding needed to exist across the organization and included everyone, from Brian, to the supervisors, to the operators and technicians. Once that understanding was established, it was followed with unwavering management consistency. In fact, consistency in interpretation and in actions had become the ARI management watchwords.

The policies, procedures, and guidelines at ARI were already documented. The breakdown came when the communication factor was added. No one had recognized the potential for gaps in manager understanding and interpretation that would result from so many recently hired managers. That led to inconsistency, which could have led to much bigger problems than just confused and unhappy employees.

Jim had gone out of his way to establish a strong partnership with Jane Donaldson in the Human Resources department. Had he not done that in the short time that he had been with Amber Rose, he might not have developed such a creative approach to resolving the lack of consistency in interpretation.

Ultimately, Amber Rose made all policies, procedures, guidelines, and expectations readily available to all employees, strategically placing reference guidelines where all employees had access. Human Resources began providing all new employees with a class on the policies, procedures, guidelines, and expectations during their first 30 days of employment. Managers went through additional training, as well.

For his part, Jim ensured that training on both interpretation and enforcement of policies, procedures, and guidelines became a part of the Supervisor Training Program that he had co-developed with Mary and Jane.

Meeting Commitments: Follow-Up and Follow-Through
Jim correctly recognized that this part of the plan really needed to start with the ARI management team. It was imperative that management role-model the traits and characteristics that they expected to see in others. In the past, Brian, Jim, Mary, and the supervisors had failed to listen, acknowledge, and close on issues that the employees had brought forward to them. Even when it meant saying "no" to a request, the employees appreciated the closure. Employees were more likely to accept negative decisions when they were properly communicated. That included communication of not only the decision itself, but also the reasons for the decision.

Jim and Mary both recognized and acknowledged that they had been guilty of not being good role models in this category.

When management wasn't willing to accept ownership or didn't provide closure on issues, it was virtually impossible to expect the company's employees to willingly commit to owning the problems and issues that they identified. It also did nothing to foster a trusting environment. Jim's goal was to create an environment in which every employee would step forward to partner in the removal of roadblocks that were hindering the performance of the factory.

Conversely, when management stepped forward to make commitments and then ensured that those commitments were met, they were creating a trusting environment. Making and meeting commitments was the best way for management to demonstrate that it could be trusted by the workforce.

Making and meeting commitments was really very easy. All that was required was for management to acknowledge when a commitment was made. As the work was being done to meet the commitment, it was important to provide updates that included expected final delivery dates. If there were changes in either the deliverable or the delivery date, those who were affected by the changes were immediately notified. Management needed to ensure that they were driving to true and complete closure, which included communication of that closure.

Day-to-Day Operations

Jim, Mary, and the supervisors had all been surprised by the size of this issue. Yet, as Darin had acknowledged, day-to-day operations were core to the very job that each of them performed. While Darin felt that they had not been doing their jobs, Mary and many of the supervisors had been overwhelmed by the enormity of the action plan. That was especially true of the action plan in support of day-to-day operations.

There were no startlingly new ideas embedded in the actions. Addressing this issue began with establishing ground rules for day-to-day operations. This seemed intuitively obvious, yet to Jim's amazement, no ground rules had previously existed. The focus of the supervisors had been on actions that would make the jobs of all the factory employees easier to do.

Jim and Mary continued to work with the supervisors, helping to establish rules and routines for everyone. This included the scheduling of breaks and lunches and ensuring that there was 100% coverage for key equipment and work areas throughout the work period. Daily 12-minute stand-up communication meetings were also held on the factory floor. These meetings were deemed to be so important that mandatory employee attendance rules were established. Jim continued to work on this area with the production supervisors long after the Winning Basics plan was fully implemented.

Efforts to make ongoing performance status visible to every employee resulted in the installation and use of automated activity counters on all equipment throughout the factory. As an assembly piece was completed and exited the equipment or work area, the piece was automatically recorded as one more unit produced for that equipment or work area. Current status was always visible to all.

Two less sophisticated tools were installed as part of the Winning Basics effort. First was the at-station tracking sheet. While these had met with mixed acceptance, they did provide a way for operators, equipment maintenance technicians, and supervisors to see exactly how well output was going during each work period. The second tool was the communication reader board. These boards were well received by the workforce. The bigger issue was gaining commitment from the supervisors to provide the required updates.

The communication boards provided a single location to communicate daily priorities, new priorities, and current performance. Employees saw the boards as they exited their work areas and as they exited the factory for the break room. Employees also saw changes that may have occurred during their breaks and lunches every time they returned to the factory floor.

Factory cleanliness was one of the unexpected factors that had impacted daily performance. Originally, the hope had been to make general factory cleanliness and housekeeping a matter of everyone's daily routine. However, it had taken a concerted effort that included the creation of formal housekeeping and cleanliness procedures, expectations, and checklists, as well as housekeeping audits to begin institutionalizing cleanliness and housekeeping. Finally, factory cleanliness and housekeeping became a matter of routine for everyone associated with the factory.

As the factory became cleaner and more organized, safety results, product quality, and total factory output also improved. By involving the workforce in the development of the factory cleanliness processes and procedures, there was immediate ownership. Everyone who toured the factory routinely ended those tours with compliments about the factory's clean, organized appearance.

Where operators and equipment maintenance technicians had before routinely planned their own break and lunch schedules, with the assumption by management that they would be planned to maximize factory performance, that was no longer the case. How could employees who were aware of neither current performance status, nor the current factory priorities, be expected to plan their breaks and lunches appropriately?

Now supervisors would formally assign break and lunch times immediately following the stand-up meetings held at the start of every shift. Later, after everyone clearly understood factory priorities and factory status, individual work groups would begin to assume ownership for this planning.

Decision-making in the factory was full of risk as long as employees didn't know the priorities or how their decisions and actions related to the factory's priorities. The key was to make goals and priorities meaningful to those who were hearing them. Employees hadn't realized how their actions affected the entire business. If employees didn't understand the ultimate impact of the tasks they performed and the decisions they made, they were likely to make the wrong decisions because they didn't realize the importance of specific tasks and actions.

For example, an employee might decide not to run a specific work order that was critical to retaining a customer. The wrong decision might result not out of maliciousness, but because the right information to make the right decision was not known.

An employee might decide to shut down a station and go to lunch without finishing the work order in process, or without getting a qualified person to continue to run the equipment. That, in turn, might cause a downstream workstation to run out of work to process, thus impacting their ability to meet output goals. The net result was that the factory might fail to meet output goals. Another often unexpected result was that as everyone rushed to work faster to recover and meet output goals, they tended to make mistakes.

Employee Training and Development

"Training costs money" was the old watch phrase in management when Jim had arrived at Amber Rose Industries. "Why spend money training people who are going to quit and go to work for our competitors?" he had heard someone say. "Let's just teach them the minimum they need to know to do the job so we can minimize training and development costs."

Knowing the status of employee training and cross-training in the factory was important to effectively running the factory. Had the factory's true training status been recognized earlier, there would have been a significant reduction in the amount of time and money necessary to fill voids. Training gaps were impacting the factory's ability to properly staff critical stations and work areas. As a result, output suffered.

Completing the right training earlier would have also potentially offered trained employees the opportunity to uncover and resolve issues before they impacted Amber Rose customers.

Jim and the "training team" had finished developing the Factory Training Plan. It wasn't fancy, but it was functional. That tool provided a framework for every factory training gap to be documented and addressed. The plan allowed every employee to see existing training gaps and know where to appropriately volunteer so they could be trained to fill the gap.

In this way, the training plan became one more tool to highlight priorities—in this case, training priorities. The plan was a visible tool available to every employee. In addition, an employee could request the training or development that he or she felt would offer career benefits.

The Factory Training Plan contained a comprehensive training plan for every employee. There was also a thorough training plan for every piece of equipment, as well as a training plan for every work area or group. Finally, there was a plan for the factory. That plan included information about upcoming new pieces of equipment, as well as general, factory-wide training needs such as the problem-solving training that every factory employee would be attending. As the Factory Training Plan came together, Jim found it easy to assess the current situation regarding trained personnel. He could also assess the status of training materials. Several gaps became apparent in training materials. Without those training materials, the quality of the training in terms of both content and consistency were in jeopardy.

Jim slipped the actions list back into its folder and leaned back in his chair with his hands behind his head. He was pleased as he contemplated the improvements in the factory since he had come to ARI. His only regret was that he'd waited so long to confront Brian. The risk was obvious: Jim could have lost his job. But the results that had been achieved since that fateful event exceeded even his most optimistic expectations.

Just as Jim had resented seeing *Demonstrate and Develop Trust and Respect* in the Management Areas of Focus, he also knew that just stating the words *self-discipline* and *shared ownership* was inadequate. Employees simply didn't trust that management promises would be carried out. They also didn't trust that management commitments would ever become reality. Management needed to take the lead and demonstrate exactly what this meant. Once that was done, a risk-taking employee or two had to be willing to take the step forward as well. When those employees stepped forward, supervisors and managers needed to reward them with recognition for taking the initiative, no matter what the outcome.

Jim had been careful to involve the entire workforce in the recovery effort. Once every employee understood that the factory was not meeting its production goals—and, more importantly, what those goals were—everyone began to focus on achieving the right results. Employees began to recognize the problems that were limiting the factory's performance, and they suggested methods for either reducing or eliminating those problems.

Jerry's leadership role within the factory had continued to develop. He had requested approval to begin attending a specialized management training certification program at the local university, and Mary had enthusiastically approved his request. In recognition of his growth and the results that he was achieving, Jerry had been identified as Mary's replacement as the factory equipment-engineering manager. This was in preparation for Mary's upcoming move into the production manager role, which Jim no longer held.

Three weeks earlier, Brian had called Jim into his office and announced that Jim would become the new factory general manager.

"By moving you into the factory manager position," Brian had explained, "I'll be able to devote my time to capturing enough business to keep the factory fully loaded and operating to its full potential. In fact, I plan to add so much business that this factory will not only need to meet 100% of its goals, but I expect that we'll soon be adding additional production shifts."

Jim gazed out his window at the rushing waterfall, trying to absorb how his prospects had turned around in such a short time. A few months earlier, he had been humiliated in front of everyone and in danger of being fired on the spot. Now he had been promoted and given additional responsibilities. The Winning Basics plan had rescued not only the factory's performance and reputation, but the futures of Jim and the other employees as well. The attitudes and day-to-day experiences of the employees had improved drastically.

Earlier that day, during a business review meeting, Brian had asked, "Jim, why did you wait so long to step forward and get us back on track?"

But that's another story . . .

Author's Comments

While most readers with any knowledge of manufacturing might suggest that Jim should have picked up sooner on the many manufacturing issues he and the others at Amber Rose Industries eventually identified, in reality it might not have been so easy. Jim came to ARI from a well-run organization. He had never been asked to address many of the issues that were present. He was also new to Amber Rose's business. While those of us who are looking in from the outside can clearly see many of the problems, it can be much harder to do so from the inside. This is especially true if you're new to the company and in the midst of transitioning to a new job.

In Jim's case, the situation was further complicated by his need to rely on Mary as his coach and mentor during his assimilation into the company. While she was known for achieving results, Mary was not a fighter. She chose the path of least resistance when Brian's inappropriate behavior continued. She offered little to Jim in terms of dealing with the situation at Amber Rose until it had already come to a head and she was ready to leave.

When Jim saw Mary taking action to leave, he recognized that without her, there was no plan of action that could successfully address the problems at ARI in a timely manner. Mary's balanced approach, her knowledge of the company's history, and her knowledge of employee feedback all became critical pieces of the puzzle that they were ultimately able to solve.

For his part, Brian represented the manager we have probably all had at one time or another. He was an excellent sales and marketing person who was trying to learn the factory. But he was learning while also fighting the fires in a factory that was not performing well. Over time, he became unable to delegate authority. Prior to Jim's arrival, previous production managers had lost their jobs due to operational errors. One of the consequences of these' mistakes was that Brian began to lose faith in the competence of others. Unfortunately, rather than allowing his experts to do their jobs, Brian's errors only made things worse. As tension mounted, Brian's ability to effectively lead diminished.

If someone at ARI had spearheaded the Winning Basics effort earlier, the events in this story would have been much different. The symptoms were there, yet no one took ownership by putting measures in place to address the root causes. Both customers and employees had been giving Jim, Mary, and Brian feedback about the issues, problems, and incidents that were negatively affecting them. Brian's tirades, Jim's newness to the company, and Mary's thoughts about moving to a new job all kept them from recognizing the actions that had to be taken.

The feedback they received early on could have been put to good use in resolving the problems, first by truly listening and understanding the nature of the problems, and then by fixing them. It should not have required a Winning Basics effort to save the company.

Amber Rose Industries
Winning Basics

A) Communication
1. All-Hands, Start-of-Shift Meetings
a) Start of Every Shift
b) Mandatory Attendance
c) Production and Equipment Supervisor Share Leadership
d) Set Agenda

2. Communication Reader Boards
a) Primary Location at Front of Factory
b) Satellite Locations within Major Work Areas
c) Hourly Updates

3. Real-time Performance Tracking and Feedback
a) At-Station Tracking Sheets
b) Hourly Updates on Information

B) Policies, Procedures, Guidelines & Expectations
1. Development, Documentation, and Communication
2. Self-Discipline and Assumed Individual Ownership

C) Meeting Commitments
1. Closure on Communications
2. Closure on Assigned Actions

D) Day-to-Day Operations
1. Quality Control
2. Management of Priority Changes
3. Break and Lunch Station Coverage Planning
4. Communication of Products and Priorities

Printed in the United States
43295LVS00002B/250-309